PROPHETS OF
HEAVEN & HELL

VIRGIL, DANTE, MILTON, GOETHE

An Introductory Essay

by

CHARLES RODEN BUXTON

NEW YORK / RUSSELL & RUSSELL

Weh! Weh!
Du hast sie zerstört,
Die schöne Welt,
Mit mächtiger Faust;
Sie stürzt, sie zerfällt!
Ein Halbgott hat sie zerschlagen!
Wir tragen
Die Trümmern ins Nichts hinüber,
Und klagen
Ueber die verlorne Schöne.
Mächtiger
Der Erdensöhne,
Prächtiger
Baue sie wieder;
In deinem Busen baue sie auf!

Geisterchor (Faust i, Act ii, Sc. 2).

FIRST PUBLISHED IN 1945

REISSUED, 1969, BY RUSSELL & RUSSELL

A DIVISION OF ATHENEUM PUBLISHERS, INC.

WITH THE PERMISSION OF CAMBRIDGE UNIVERSITY PRESS

L. C. CATALOG CARD NO: 68-25070

PRINTED IN THE UNITED STATES OF AMERICA

CONTENTS

INTRODUCTION

THIS book was written during the last two years of my husband's life, but the theme of it had long haunted his mind. Outwardly his life was devoted to politics, especially to international politics, but the springs of his action went deep, and his last writings as given in these chapters help to show whence he drew inspiration for a life of unremitting struggle. Some of his friends have regretted that he felt the claim of politics to be supreme, and that he had not chosen instead a literary or academic career. To literature and especially to poetry he turned, however, at all times for recreation and refreshment, and being a good linguist the field of his inspiration was a wide one. In Virgil especially he found the best companion for his journeys, or the solace for desolate hours. Even in that peak of excitement and suspense in a parliamentary election when the candidates are required to attend the counting of the votes which determine their fate, the *Aeneid* would be produced from his pocket and capture his attention.

The present essay was envisaged by him as introductory to a much larger book to which he had hoped to devote a number of years, and in which the same theme would have been worked out in an intensive study of the four poet-prophets. He liked to think that his *literarisch-geschichtliche Aufgabe* was to help in 'rehabilitating the long poem'.

A number of his notes in connection with the book afford interesting illustration of his own line of thought. Thus he asks himself, 'What is the reality behind the ideas of "Heaven and Hell"?' 'Heaven is blessedness, salvation, reunion with the Whole.... Unity of humanity, unity with the dead of all ages and with the future generations,—this is the unity which inspires me;—other unities don't.'

His death occurred in December 1942, after three years of increasing ill health (due, as I believe, to the agony of mind caused him by the war). Two years before the end his friend Lord Ponsonby wrote to him: 'How profitably you are using your enforced retirement! There are two sets of readers to whom you will appeal. Those who, like myself, profoundly believe in the wholeness of life, who discard the time sequence and hold to a sense of proportion which, within the whole, makes every moment of high significance. They will be encouraged by finding that these four great minds endorse such views. The other section, who have already a good knowledge of the four poets, will be interested to have pointed out to them the profound, all-embracing outlook which moved these poets to write as they did. . . . Let us be hopeful! For in the cycles which the whole contains, greater light succeeds darkness, seemingly at long intervals if measured by the misleading Time measure, but shrinking in the so-called Past into their proper proportions and, while they last, assisted or delayed by the tiniest effort of the humblest mortal.'

My husband did not live to complete the last two chapters of his book (but I have finished them as far as possible in accordance with his notes), nor to make any final additions or changes in the rest of the book. The translation on the final page was not included in his MS. but has been added by myself. Three of the chapters have appeared in shortened form in the *Contemporary Review*, and my thanks are due to the Editor for permission to reprint them. I would like also to thank Mr R. C. Trevelyan for his kindness in going through the proofs.

DOROTHY F. BUXTON

AUTHOR'S PREFACE

THE aim of this book is to commend the study of the four great poems with which it deals to a far wider circle of readers than they reach to-day.

This, I believe, can best be done by showing what it is that the writers set out to do—their main purpose, to which the story itself, and all the beauty, and all the fascinating detail, is subordinated. That purpose (whether conscious or not, and whether contemplated in advance or not will be discussed below) was to embody in a single work of art a connected view of life as a whole.

Once they are regarded from this standpoint, their similarities will be realised, and the reader will at once see why, in this book, the four poems are treated together. It is a fact—though to me a strange one—that they have never been so treated before.

Feeling this unity between them, I have steeped myself, for many years past, not in the innumerable things that have been written about them, but in what they actually said. Rather than browse at large among the vast and tempting fields of literature, I have, in leisure hours and on holidays, to some extent 'specialised' in these four poems.

This has been the main intellectual diversion during an uninterrupted career of 'practical politics'. If such a career seems to some a disqualification, I would say in reply that I do not think it is altogether so. It is not generally recognised that every one of the four poets went through a similar experience, except Virgil—and he knew it through contact with leading politicians. Milton, above all, was conscious of the awful struggle involved in the setting aside of 'delightful studies' and great artistic aims to 'embark in a troubled sea of noises and hoarse disputes', to engage in a struggle with men of wholly different aims in life, to forsake 'learned pains for unlearned drudgery' (*Reason of Church Government urged against Prelaty*, Bk II, 1642). He little thought at the outset that his voyage on the 'troubled sea' would consume nearly twenty years of the prime of life. None of the great commentators, as far as I know, has had any experience of this kind. None of them has known the effort required to shift the focus continually from exasperating details—from 'circumstances' as Milton called them—to great and comprehensive ideas, or felt the sting of the problem as to the relative values of the life of thought and of action, with its ever recurring personal issue. None of them has known the sense of urgency which is instilled by the constant need of immediate action, whether in small things or great. Still less have they known what it is to be called upon to express oneself, at any moment, by hook or by crook, to large miscellaneous audiences. I believe these experiences had much to do with forming the special genius of the four poets.

A book of the kind I have attempted seems to me to be all the more needed, because in our time the poems have fallen into relative disfavour. For reasons which will be discussed below, the long poem as such is not popular; and the few who read these four poems, or any of them, know them only in fragments—the first four books of the *Aeneid*, the first Cantica (the *Inferno*) of the *Divine Comedy*, the first four books of *Paradise Lost*, and the First Part of *Faust*. Virgil has, in addition, owing to an unfortunate development in our classical education during the past hundred years, become mainly the happy hunting-ground of schoolmasters, and the bugbear of schoolboys.

At the same time, it is right to ask: 'Why should we be urged to study these particular poems in a new way, and no longer in fragments? Why study them at all? Life is short; leisure is limited; we have innumerable books, far more than our fathers had, which invite us to study them.' It is not an unreasonable question to ask. By all means let us continue to ignore them, if they are not in fact unique, and if they do not stand high in the list of human achievements. Do not let us be slaves to past reputations, however great they may have been. Let us decide for ourselves.

The book itself is an attempt to answer this question. But some preliminary suggestion of the reasons for an affirmative reply may be given here. We cannot ignore the fact that men at all times, until our own, have rated them above most others. Why was this? They came into the world on an equality with many others. *Paradise Lost*, indeed, had the whole current of its time—literary as well as political—against it. Dryden was the dictator; rhyming tragedies were the vogue; Puritanism was at a discount; Milton had lately been in danger of his life; solemn blank verse lent itself to the sneers of a public among whom Butler's *Hudibras* was the latest rage.

At the times at any rate when the three later of our poems appeared no one was predisposed to like them above all others. Why did they, then, having first seized the attention of contemporaries, continue for generations to stand out in men's minds as supremely great? I only suggest this question, without at present answering it. A reasonable respect for our forefathers, if nothing else, would dispose us at least to put the question, before we decide to dismiss the study of the poems altogether. If we fail to admire certain great poets or writers, let us be ready to believe that 'we are dull', and not that the world has been 'imposed upon'.

For myself, I may, perhaps, in a Preface, express my enthusiasms more familiarly than in the body of the book; and I would add that I find in these poems, no matter how often I return to them, inexhaustible fountains of beauty and wisdom. Such they have been to generations of men and women. Such, I am convinced, they might be to the men and women of our time.

Those who feel an inclination to read them afresh, and from a new point of view, should not be deterred by supposing that some special qualifications are needed—great learning or unusual gifts. Apart from a general education, what is essential to those who would appreciate them is that, however specialised their occupation or their studies may be, they should still retain an interest in life as a whole, and in discovering for themselves some adequate explanation of it.

One thing often believed to be essential—a knowledge of the languages concerned—deserves some examination. Not to know the language is, of course, a serious loss. But the cliché about poetry being 'untranslatable' is a mark of the super-refined—if not a mask for self-conceit. On the one hand it is a truism; but on the other it is a misleading fallacy. Much depends here on the purpose we have in view in our study. The inherent beauty of the language is, of course, lost; but if the purpose is the wider one which is here suggested, the language falls into its proper place as one only, perhaps not the most important one, of the elements deserving our study. I am not suggesting that the language is a mere sheath or skin, which can be stripped off, and leave the arrangement, the disposition of parts, the dramatic qualities, the philosophy, the history, completely unaffected. The poem as it came from the author's hand is a complete thing, not analysable; for entire and perfect appreciation the language is necessary. All I am maintaining is that, short of perfect appreciation, it contains other elements which make the study well worth pursuing. And the more perfect poetry is, the more easily it is appreciated when transposed into another language and read by a foreigner.

I would add that, in the case of Virgil and Milton, the loss is far greater than in that of either Dante or Goethe. Virgil and Milton are, perhaps, the world's supreme artists in language. The language is a more vital part of the complete whole. It is partly due to this that Milton is so little appreciated on the Continent. Even to English readers, his language is so unique and individual as to require special study.

Even among men and women of little education, there is more power of appreciating such poems than is generally realised. There is often found among them (and I speak from experience) a keen enjoyment of certain aspects of these poems, mainly two things of which little notice is taken by commentators—the splendid rhetoric of the speeches, and the prolonged outpouring of magnificent and stately language. The popularity of Shakespeare, and still more of the Bible, is evidence of this. The Bible would never have attained and held its position in English life, if the wonderful company whom King James brought together in 1611 had not made an appeal to this powerful literary instinct—little as the ardent Methodist or Baptist may be conscious of the fact. A noteworthy parallel to the case of our Bible may be found in the perennial appeal of Schlegel's masterly version of Shakespeare to the people of Germany—a more striking example, if the truth were told, than the much-vaunted but archaic and uncouth rendering of the Bible by Luther. The special value of the long poem, with simpler people, is that volume and amplitude are part of the appeal. It is not without meaning that Dante's praise of Virgil refers to the 'wide river of speech' which the Roman poet 'poured forth'—*che spande di parlar sì largo fiume.*

There is one condition of appreciating these poems, which should be frankly faced in advance, for to ignore it would lead to serious disappointment. The modern habit of reading in 'snippets', promoted by our newspapers, is so deeply engrained that the power of holding a comprehensive whole in the mind is much weakened in many omnivorous readers. It is not an easy task which I am suggesting. It requires a considerable degree of effort and application at the outset. It will need the careful study of a commentary as well as the text, and, if the poem is read in the original, some use of a grammar and a dictionary. It is necessary, however, that the poems should be read, once at least, as rapidly as may be, and without reference to the commentaries' notes. One needs first to obtain some grasp of the poem as a whole; close study, and the slow reading it involves, must come later. I am convinced, however, that those who make the effort required for the appreciation of such long poems will gain something precious in life.

Some of the tests applied to these poems in the past are not accepted by us moderns as important. We do not ask whether the story is a true one or not. We do not ask whether it is a good story, because we have thousands of stories far better, far more exciting, far more skilfully woven by writers trained in the school of the modern novel. We do not ask what past critics, judging by other standards than ours, have thought of them—though the fact, as I have just said, that they were universally accepted as great, is in itself an important piece of evidence.

The tests we apply to-day—the questions we ask—are different; and this, in itself, seems to me a matter worth considering, though none of the commentators have consciously considered it. The Latin notes of the first great modern commentator on Virgil, Heyne, towards the end of the eighteenth century, answered adequately the questions then asked by his readers; but the answers are now painfully obvious, and the things in which we are interested are not even referred to. Such examples illustrate a much wïder consideration, which has been much in my mind. Is it not a good excuse for the writer of a new book, when so many exist already, that these poems need to be interpreted afresh to each generation, according to the tests it applies?

I take it that we want to know mainly three things.

(1) What inherent beauty do we find here, whether of poetry, or drama, or spectacle, which other works do not display in an equal degree?

(2) Next, since all our thinking to-day is dominated by the idea of evolution, what light do they throw on the development of human civilisation, and in particular of our Western civilisation?

(3) And lastly, and more generally, do they contain anything of importance which it concerns us, here and now, to know or to feel?

Each one of these questions will be answered in the course of this book. Whether the answers are adequate or not, the reader must judge. Of one thing, however, I am convinced; he will feel a sense of something great. Mere greatness may, of course, be forbidding, even repulsive. But on the other hand it may be irresistible, absorbing—differentiating such poems as these from others.

I can only say that, to me at least, they seem a profitable study for such hours of leisure, be they many or few, as we may have at command in these troubled days. In this 'little vigil that remains', as Dante calls it:

> A questa tanto picciola vigilia
> Dei vostri sensi, ch' è del rimanente—

it seems wise to direct our thoughts to momentous issues; and among all the various achievements of the human spirit, to choose those which, as single and separate works of art, stand out above the rest by the magnitude of their scope, and the grandeur of their aim.

Chapter I

THE SUBJECT

I

In the course of European history, four great works emerge which belong to a class apart. They are the *Aeneid*, the *Divine Comedy*, *Paradise Lost* and *Faust*. On the exact position of Virgil, Dante, Milton and Goethe among the greatest poets—a question, after all, of no great importance—I shall not attempt to pronounce. But they stand above the rest in one particular characteristic—the completeness of the scope of their poems. It is in this aspect, fundamentally, that they are viewed and handled in the book that follows. This is the theme that underlies all else that will be said of them. What chiefly unites them in a brotherhood of greatness is that each presents, in a single picture, a view of the Universe as a whole. Man's life here on earth is what primarily interests them; the story is a story of Man's pilgrimage—the evils that beset his path, his strivings, his duties, his hopes, the possibilities of his salvation. But, unlike the modern adherents of 'secular religions' such as German National Socialism and Russian Communism, they see Man against a background vaster than himself. They do not regard Man's needs and interests—whether as an individual or as a member of a society—as the test of what is right or wrong, true or untrue, beautiful or ugly. They do not regard his possibilities of salvation as being fulfilled in a Kingdom of Earth, his own creation. They see his present in the light of his past, and of his future; in the light of something outside him, independent of him, the Eternal, the Absôlute. They recognise the problem of Evil, and the problem of Salvation, as requiring for their comprehension that some account shall be taken of the whole Universe. Hence the title of this book adopts the old terminology of Hell and Heaven. Phrases such as 'Hell's depth and Heaven's utmost height' are still, in the ears of Englishmen at any rate, living expressions; and it is difficult to find others at once brief and significant.

It will be seen from this initial statement that, in the pages which follow, attention is directed to the main subject of each poem, rather than to the beauty of single passages. I have not forgotten that they are poems, and that they rank among the most famous works of literature. A chapter will be devoted to their purely artistic aspect; another to their place in history. At the same time, it is their main subject which is the essential matter, and in order to grasp this, it is desirable to read, once at least, each poem as a whole, continuously. This was what our forefathers, before the nineteenth century at any rate, did habitually; they read them as they would read a contemporary poem, such as, say, the *Faerie Queene* or the *Dunciad*.

The point needs making, because at the present time these poems are seldom studied as wholes. By a curious coincidence, it is in each case the first part which is most widely known. The majority of readers, when they think or speak of the work, in reality mean this part only. To them, the *Aeneid* means little more than the story of the sack of Troy, and the love of Aeneas for the Carthaginian queen—just 'episodes', in the original sense of the word. For one reader who knows the whole *Divine Comedy*, ten know something about the Inferno. In Milton, it is the debates of the rebel angels in Hell, and the first descriptions of Paradise before the Fall, which stand for *Paradise Lost*. While it is a commonplace that *Faust* means the ever-popular drama of Faust's temptation and Gretchen's ruin, the second part is dismissed as 'unintelligible'. Attention is rarely directed, as it will be in this book, to the real subject of each poem—the poet's main idea and purpose; the conception which he made it his life's work to embody in a masterpiece of art.

A further similarity which distinguishes these poets from others is the form in which their picture of the world is presented. We do not infer it from a series of writings, one illustrating one aspect, and another another; it is not given in fragments, but in a single poem. And the work is, apart from its content, a great and famous work of art. It is not a treatise; it is a story or 'myth', appealing primarily to the imagination.

The poet, who makes the Universe the subject of his poem, undertakes a work so supremely difficult and complicated that without an extraordinary, an apparently miraculous combination of powers and sympathies, he must ignominiously fail. That is why, in 2000 years or more, only four men have emerged who were capable of bearing the burden, and accomplishing the colossal task. Such a poet must cover the dry bones of intellectual formulation with flesh and blood; he must convey, to the mass of ordinary men and women, some kind of impression of the whole of life, in all its aspects; he must make them feel that they are concerned in what he is saying, and that he is giving them guidance in the conduct of life; he must engage their interest and attention by means of what is readable and exciting. This is the method of imagination; he must not only grasp the whole, but embody it in an image, a picture; a new creation, with a thousand elements fused into one, with a life of its own.

Returning from the form to the substance of the poems, we note that each sums up, in a degree approaching completeness, the civilisation of an important epoch in history. We see embodied, one after another, the whole knowledge and thought of the Augustan period at Rome;

of the Middle Ages; of the reintegration of Protestant Europe after the confusions following the Reformation; of the Modern Age, which is usually dated from 1789. And we see, in particular, that the audience to which all the poems are addressed is not a country or nation, but the world—Humanity as a whole. It was indeed inevitable that, regarding Man's life, as they did, in one comprehensive view, as a part of a larger whole, these poets should cease to interest themselves in such minor distinctions as those of nationality. Even the *Aeneid*, though outwardly the record of the foundation of Rome, indicates a form of polity to be applied, under Roman inspiration, to the whole known world; and Dante reproduces this idea when he makes Justinian, the codifier of the Roman Law, the spokesman of the Empire in Paradise—an Empire which he conceives as continuous with the 'Holy' Roman Empire of his own day. Julius Caesar obtained command 'nigh the time when all Heaven willed to bring the world back to its own serene mood'. The Empire (imaged as the Eagle in the *Paradiso*) 'set the world in peace'; 'governed the world beneath the shadow of its sacred wings'; and its destiny was to give the world Justice. Twice Justinian speaks of 'the living Justice which inspires me' (*la viva giustizia che mi spira*), and denounces even the Ghibellines (Dante's own party) for divorcing Justice from the sacred emblem (*la giustizia e lui diparte*). Its function is to impose, protect, and foster Justice. It was 'by the will of the Primal Love' that he codified the Roman Law (*per voler del primo Amor ch' io sento*). 'God of his grace inspired me with the high task, and I gave myself wholly to it.'

The culture of these poets, too, includes the best that they knew of other peoples than their own. Virgil draws upon the conquered Greeks and the half-Phoenician, half-African civilisation of Carthage, the hereditary foe of

Rome. Dante draws upon the Arabs, the enemies of the Cross; Milton upon all the nations of Europe, as well as on the Jewish and Pagan civilisation. Goethe absorbed all the culture of the French and the Italians, and as soon as he learned about it, the atmosphere and the poetry of Persia and the East. There is no trace of hostility or contempt for other peoples as such.

But while they include other civilisations in their universal sympathy, it is the civilisation of Europe to which, above all, they have themselves contributed. Each poem has passed, in large measure, into the language and thought of subsequent generations. The words, the images, the characters, the incidents have become part of the common stock from which European literature inspires and refreshes itself, and the European mind is nourished. Nor are they mere mouthpieces. These poems, by their widespread influence, are themselves among the sources of our Western civilisation.

As for the personalities of the poets themselves, here again they stand apart from some others who are accounted great. We are not to look here for anything primitive, anything perfectly fresh and spontaneous and unsophisticated. Each was essentially a highly civilised man, 'upon whom the ends of all the ages had come', a man of the widest culture and experience.

Nor was this all; he was one who not merely lived the inner life of the artist or the seer, but was intimately acquainted with the public and political affairs of his time. Three out of the four were what we should call 'practical politicians'; the fourth, Virgil, was in close touch with politics through his intimacy with the leading statesmen.

Above all, each had reflected profoundly on the main problems of existence; and his broad human sympathies inspired him with a keen desire to teach, to communicate his ripe wisdom to his fellow-men.

In the next chapter, I shall discuss at greater length how far it is justifiable to use the term 'prophet' in describing them. Here it is enough to say that, in each case, there was something more than the urge of the teacher to help his fellows; there was, behind this, some sense of a responsibility to do so, some consciousness of a 'mission'.

Lastly, each poet may be said to have looked on his great poem as the main concern of his life. In the event, Virgil devoted approximately ten years to his, Dante sixteen intermittently and six wholly; Milton at least nine; while Goethe spread the writing of *Faust*, with long intervals, over at least fifty years of his crowded life. And it is no mere coincidence but highly significant as illuminating the psychology of the poet, that in each case the idea of such a poem captured the poet's imagination at an early age; there was some presentiment of future greatness, to be crowned by some single outstanding achievement.

Virgil wrote in his *Georgics* (III, 8 sqq.), long before the *Aeneid* was begun, that he contemplated erecting a marble temple, which he describes at length, at his native Mantua. We find, as he proceeds, that he is speaking of a great poem, celebrating Augustus, and tracing his family—the Julian—back to its origin in the founders of Troy. It is to deal also with a descent to the world of the dead; and the singling out of this incident tends to support the view, which will be expressed below, that the Sixth Book of the *Aeneid* is the pivot on which the whole poem turns.

Dante, in his *Vita Nuova*, writing of Beatrice after her death in 1290, when he was twenty-five years old, writes of the 'wonderful vision' of Beatrice in Paradise, 'in which I saw things which made me resolve not to speak more of this blessed one until such time as I should be able to indite more worthily of her. . . . If it shall be the pleasure of Him, by whom all things live, that my life continue for some years, I hope to say of her that which never hath been said of any woman.'

Milton, writing in 1642 (his thirty-fourth year), describes at length (in his *Reason of Church Government urged against Prelaty*) the idea of a great poem which should be the main work of his life. Such an idea had already been adumbrated in his thirtieth year in the Latin *Epistle to Manso* (1638) and in the *Epitaphium Damonis* (1638), an elegy on his college friend Diodati. He suggests that it was the high opinion of his poetry expressed by his Italian friends (on his journey to Italy) which first gave definite shape to this idea. The poem at that time was to deal with King Arthur and the Round Table; though within a few years Milton had determined that no less vast a canvas than the Universe, and no less a hero than the Son of God, would suffice to fulfil his hopes. He excuses himself for enlarging, in such an unexpected place as a political pamphlet, on 'what the mind at home, in the spacious circuits of her musing, hath liberty to propose to herself, though of highest hope and hardest attempting'. It is a proof, he says, of the overmastering call of politics that it involved the temporary sacrifice of 'the pursuit of no less hopes than these'. He speaks of the 'inward prompting' which, at a much earlier period, 'grew daily upon me, that by labour and intense study...I might perhaps leave something so written to aftertimes, as they should not willingly let it die'; and he goes on to pass in review the various possible forms—the epic, the drama, and so on.

Goethe only differed from the rest in that his imagination seized first upon the actual story of the historical *Faust*, and the legends to which it gave rise, and only gradually came to conceive it as the vehicle for his picture of human life. Evidence of extraordinary interest is provided by the *Urfaust*, the original draft of about 1775, his twenty-sixth year—a document only discovered in 1887, fifty-five years after his death. The story itself is still the main interest. But he himself told Eckermann (*Conversations of Goethe*) that he had had the more philosophical Second Part 'in his head' for fifty years, that is since 1779. By the time that the completed Part I was published in 1808, he had added the *Prologue in Heaven* and the *Prologue on the Stage*, showing that by that date *Faust* had become the basis for something much greater, a pilgrimage 'from Heaven through the Earth to Hell'. The poem was not completed till 1831.

II

The reader who has followed this brief sketch of the common qualities uniting Virgil, Dante, Milton and Goethe, will recognise that these qualities are important enough to place them in a class apart. These four poets belong to a certain *type*, but also they occupy a certain position in literature and history. The reader will see why other famous works, which might at first sight be thought to belong to that class, are here excluded. None of them exhibit these particular qualities in combination.

Homer, for example, if we are to speak at all of a single author of the Homeric poems, can hardly be said to present us with a connected view of the universe; or if he does, it is one of so primitive a character that it does not count among the conceptions that have had an enduring influence on our civilisation. Moreover, neither the *Iliad* nor the *Odyssey*, which differ so widely from one another, stands out obviously as the single work which could be placed side by side with the four poems I have named.

The Bible at once suggests itself as a great source—some would say, the greatest of the sources—from which our civilisation is derived. But the Bible is a collection of writings covering a large part of Jewish history, and no one book in the collection could be singled out as the type or representative of the whole, not even the *Psalms*, nor *Job*, nor *Isaiah*, nor the *Revelation*.

Shakespeare, it might be said, is the greatest of poets; he plumbs the depths of human nature; he sums up the whole culture of an age, the age of the Renaissance. But here again we are confronted with a mass of separate writings; and no one of them, not *Hamlet* itself, could claim a place, by its comprehensiveness, among those named. It may indeed be questioned—it is a standing subject of controversy—whether any connected view of things emerges from the plays, the sonnets, and the poems, if they are read as a whole—and if we further assume (as the present writer, incidentally, is not prepared to assume) a single authorship for the whole.

Some other famous poems might at first sight be suggested as belonging to the class which contains the *Aeneid*, the *Divine Comedy*, *Paradise Lost* and *Faust*. But in every case it will be found that they do not fulfil the conditions. Lucretius, for example, who writes on the *Nature of Things*, does not embody his conception in a story or myth, and this is perhaps the reason why his great philosophical poem has never made the appeal, or exercised the influence throughout the centuries, of the *Aeneid*.

There remains the list of those who have used the same form, broadly speaking, as Virgil, Dante, Milton and Goethe—viz. the recognised writers of epics, Lucan, Statius, Ariosto, Tasso, Camoens. Some Germans might claim a place for Wagner's *Ring*; some Englishmen, a place for Spenser's *Faerie Queene* or, perhaps with more justice, for Hardy's *Dynasts*. Of these it may be said with confidence that in one respect, at least, none of them can bear comparison with the poets who form the subject of this essay. They have exercised no comparable influence on the culture of Europe. If Oedipus has become a household word, this is due to the Greek dramatists, and not to the *Thebaid*. If Roland the Paladin has become the type of youthful bravery and chivalry, it is not from the *Orlando Furioso* that he has earned his halo. But apart from this special consideration, no reader, who makes a dispassionate survey of these famous writers, would claim for any one of them the title of a prophet of Earth, Hell, and Heaven.

It is not possible, in so brief a survey as this chapter affords, to indicate the richness and variety of the theme here outlined. In concentrating attention on the common features which characterise all the four poems, it has been necessary to adopt, for the sake of brevity, the method of abstraction; and to indicate those common features in the baldest and most general terms. Space has not permitted even an allusion to the vast range of qualities and powers and interests which are the peculiar glory of each separate poem, merely because they are not common features of all of them; nor any hint of the great glow of illumination which each one sheds on the age in which the poet lived. Regarded merely as a study of a certain stage in the history of the European mind, each of them is, of course, capable of forming the study of a lifetime. Or again, if some particular aspect of life is taken as the starting-point of our thought—say Theology, or Art, or Science, or Political Philosophy, or Ethics, or Jurisprudence—each poet will be found to have a distinctive conception of his own, which it is useful to compare or contrast with those of the other three. To some of these topics reference will be made in succeeding chapters. But enough perhaps has now been said to commend our theme to the reader.

Chapter II

POETS OR PROPHETS?

The mission of the prophet is usually surrounded by an atmosphere of mysteriousness, not favourable to careful enquiry. But for the purpose of this book, which claims for Virgil, Dante, Milton and Goethe a high place among the world's prophets as well as among its poets, it is essential to see clearly how they conceived their function, and to read their works in the light of that conception. I have spoken of their great poems as works of art; but it is evident at once that they are not merely works of art. By that expression I understand a work in which the writer had in fact no motive except the artistic; to produce a thing of beauty, and thereby to give delight to himself and to other men. These poets all regarded themselves as something more than mere artists in this sense. What was this 'something more'? That is the subject of this chapter.

To Virgil and Dante the problem here raised would have had no meaning whatever. In their day, the spheres of the ethical and didactic on the one hand, and of the aesthetic on the other, had not been differentiated. The idea of Truth and Goodness and Beauty as three purposes which might be pursued separately, an idea so familiar to us to-day, was unknown. Philosophy has since advanced, by steps which cannot be retraced, in definition and classification. The map of our world of thought is covered by so many more delineations that we find it hard to realise a world where vast spaces were left entirely blank. Neither Virgil nor Dante, however, whether they could conceive such a thing as 'mere' Art or not, looked on his work as limited to that sphere. Virgil and Dante took it for granted that fine craftsmanship, and the moving appeal of subtly woven words, were beautiful and desirable things. Virgil delights in describing works of craftsmanship, such as embroidery or carved wooden bowls. But neither he nor Dante ever dreamed that Art could be an exclusive mistress, a goal to which all else could be subordinated. On the contrary, the great poets who people Elysium in Virgil's tale are the good or pious bards, the *pii vates*. The poet was also conceived as a man of deep knowledge, and the ideal of the learned poet, *doctus poeta*, persisted for centuries. If this was true of the Graeco-Roman civilisation, which devoted endless pains to securing artistic perfection, much more was it true of the mediaeval period, for then the words and images of the poet, the 'artful voice' of the singer, the lovely colours and lines of the architect, sculptor or painter, were thought of primarily as symbols of things unseen, great truths seeking utterance through the thin veil of the external. St Thomas Aquinas's definition of beauty is narrow—completeness, proportion, and brilliant colour—and he assumes that these are means to be used, not ends in themselves. The admiration of the later Middle Ages, as far as we can judge, was reserved for the skilful rendering of details on the one hand, and on the other for the sense of sublimity and sanctity which the artist could produce.

Dante had, indeed, what might be called a theory of aesthetics, as might be expected from one who studied so minutely the whole question of language. But it completely subordinated Art to the teaching of spiritual truths. All mortal things are like wax, which takes the imprint of the heavenly stamp, though not always perfectly, like the artist who has the practice of his art, but a hand that trembles— '*Che ha l' abito dell' arte, e man che trema*' (*Par.* XIII, 78).

The characteristic of the 'sweet new style', the *dolce stil' nuovo* of which he claims to have been, with his friends Guido Cavalcanti and Cino da Pistoia, one of the first exponents, was that the poet should look into his own heart and write what he found there. 'I am one who, when Love inspires me, take note, and go setting it forth after the fashion which he dictates within me.'

> Io mi son un che, quando
> Amor mi spira, noto, ed a quel modo
> Che ditta dentro, vo significando.
>
> (*Purg.* XXIV, 52.)

And what does love 'dictate within me'? All degrees of love are inspired by the soul's desire for union with God. Dante's love, the union of his soul with a gentle lady, 'in whom the divine light strongly shone to me', directs his thoughts to the divine, which shows itself through nature and through human reason alike. The function of his art is to set forth divine things. The idea of human love becomes transformed into the idea of that heavenly wisdom of which, in the *Paradiso*, Beatrice becomes the symbol. Dante was led, it seems, away from Religion to Philosophy, and Beatrice, in the *Divine Comedy*, when she reproaches him for his backsliding, tells him that while she was on earth, she 'sustained him with my countenance; showing my youthful eyes to him, I led him with me, turned to the right goal'.

> Il sostenni col mio volto;
> Mostrando gli occhi giovinetti a lui,
> Meco il menava, in dritta parte volto.
>
> (*Purg.* XXX, 121.)

By Milton's time, the process of differentiation had gone so much further that we find him, in his untroubled youth, in practice if not in theory, making pure Beauty his goddess. In a Latin letter to his intimate College friend Charles Diodati, he writes:

What besides God has resolved concerning me I know not, but this at least—He has instilled into me, if into anyone, a vehement love of the beautiful. Not with so much labour . . . is

Ceres said to have sought her daughter Proserpina, as it is my habit day and night to seek for this idea of the beautiful, as for a certain image of supreme beauty, through all the forms and faces of things (for many are the shapes of things divine) and to follow it as it leads me on, by some sure traces which I seem to recognise.

But that stage soon passed, and he decided, with his habitual definiteness and determination, that the purpose of Art was simply to serve the building up of an ideal state, and the instruction and elevation of the human spirit. It is all the more a testimony to his amazing powers that, in spite of this theoretical subordination of Art, he should have become the greatest artist in poetry to whom England has given birth.

As for Goethe, the mental attitude is wholly different; yet it is not less distant from that of the 'pure artist'. Nothing could be further from the truth than the opinion, once current in this country, that Goethe dwelt apart in a *tour d'ivoire*, an isolated aesthetic world such as Tennyson pictures in the *Palace of Art*. Goethe never dreamed of separating Art from the other activities of life. It is true that few great writers have accorded to it so high a place in their scheme of things; in the Second Part of *Faust* a whole act—that which describes the meeting of Faust and Helen, and forms the centre of the drama—deals with the relation of modern to ancient Art, and more widely, with the relation of Beauty—all Beauty—to the individual life and to civilisation generally. But it is also true that he describes himself as receiving the gift of Poetry from the hands, not of Beauty, but of Truth—

Der Dichtung Schleier aus der Hand der Wahrheit;

and Truth, in the vision, reproaches him for devoting himself to her in solitary worship, and will not bestow the gift until he has cried out that the good in him is for other men, that he will no longer enjoy it alone; 'Why did I seek so longingly for the way, if it were not that I should point it out to my brothers?'

> Warum sucht ich den Weg so sehnsuchtsvoll,
> Wenn ich ihn nicht den Brüdern zeigen soll?
> (*Zueignung*, the dedication to his collected poems.)

It is evident, then, that all four poets are something more than 'pure artists'; they are all aware of some power outside themselves, of which they are the mouthpieces. And there is another characteristic in which they all share. They are deeply in earnest. They are concerned with the problem of 'how to live'; their primary interest is ethical. They feel moved to communicate the wisdom they have won; to be teachers of men. They belong to the class which the great Italian critic Benedetto Croce has described by the name of *poeta-vate*, the poet-prophet; 'he who, animated by a strong ethical spirit, proposes to his fellow-citizens, to his fellow-countrymen, or to men in general, a direction to follow in life'.

But there is much more that we would fain know. How, for instance, did they conceive the power of which they were the mouthpieces, and how did they think that it operated in them? Every artist who has also the habit of cool reflexion must, at times, stand apart from his work, and picture himself in a certain relation to his fellow-men, a certain attitude towards his special function as artist. These poets did so. And it is interesting, and in the present case especially useful, to trace the shades of difference.

Virgil held the Stoic idea of the one divine power which rules the Universe—Jupiter, in popular language, and behind Jupiter, *Fatum* or *Fata*. This is the spirit, the mind (*spiritus*, *mens*) which animates all things, and gives them fiery life—

> Igneus est ollis vigor et caelestis origo.

It breathes into all living creatures, inspiring individuals and moulding the destiny of states. It allots to each man his special place and task, which he must not desert, as a soldier must not desert his post.

Virgil presents a curious anomaly. He was a supreme artist in poetry, down to the last refinement in technique; yet none of the four poets named, as far as we can judge, subordinated his art more completely to his duty; his task as teacher and inspirer of his fellow-countrymen. His one explicit reference to art is a contemptuous one. In the peroration of his final speech in Elysium, Anchises exhorts the Romans that are to be to practise those powers in which they naturally excel—those of the efficient soldier and far-sighted statesman. 'These shall be thy arts!' And he contrasts the Greeks, whose glory is in their sculptors in brass and marble, their professors of rhetoric, and their philosophers (*Aeneid*, VI, 847):

> Others shall beat out the breathing bronze to softer lines, I believe it well; shall draw living lineaments from the marble; they shall be better pleaders in the courts; their pencil shall trace the movements of the heavenly bodies; they shall tell the stars in their rising. Be it thy charge, O Roman, to rule the nations in thine empire; these shall be thy arts: to lay down the law of peace; to be merciful to the vanquished; to war down the proud.
>
> (Based on J. W. Mackail's translation.)

> Excudent alii spirantia mollius aera,
> Credo equidem, vivos ducent de marmore vultus,
> Orabunt causas melius, coelique meatus
> Describent radio, et surgentia sidera dicent;
> Tu regere imperio populos, Romane, memento;
> Hae tibi erunt artes; pacisque imponere morem,
> Parcere subjectis, et debellare superbos.

Dante, who was keenly alive to the wonders of Virgil's art, but who entered also into his whole mind with a loving sympathy which has never been surpassed, regarded him as first and foremost the teacher, the 'wise guide', 'the sea of all wisdom', 'the honour of every science and every art'; indeed, the symbol of Human Wisdom, as Beatrice was of the Divine. Just as Virgil writes his *Georgics* to promote Augustus's policy of settling small farmers on the land, so he writes his *Aeneid* to promote the ideal—the Roman ideal—which he regards as underlying and glorifying that policy. He is rightly spoken of as 'the prophet of Rome'. In the solemn invocation to the Muse which begins the crowning stage of his narrative (*Aeneid*, VII, 37) he calls himself the *vates*, the bard or prophet.

In the Middle Ages, indeed, he was regarded as a prophet in the popular sense—one who foretells the future. It was thought that in his fourth *Eclogue* he definitely prophesied the birth of Christ. St Paul is described in an early hymn as doing honour to his tomb; and a statue of him appears among the saints in the cathedral of Zamora, in Castile. It is the custom of scholars to smile at this naïve belief, but it must be admitted that there is still something mysterious about this singular little poem, in which the birth of an expected child is to herald the Golden Age; an idea entirely unfamiliar to the Roman poets, who placed the Golden Age in the past, not in the future. Virgil adopts the Jewish attitude, and, moreover, he describes the Age in figures and phrases identical with those of Isaiah. Professor Mayor and others have traced his possible knowledge of Jewish imagery to the Sibylline Books, into which the Jews of Alexandria had imported some of their own prophetic language among oracular utterances which then had a wide popularity.

In the minds of Dante and Milton, the power so vaguely conceived by Virgil has become the Christian personal

God. But there is a marked difference. To Dante, God is mainly the source of all truth and the power towards which all things are drawn 'through the great sea of being' (*per lo gran mar del essere*); the Love 'which moves the sun and the other stars'—

> L' Amor che muove 'l Sole e l' altre stelle.
>
> (*Paradiso* XXXIII, 145.)

Dante's main aim was to set out God's purpose with regard to sin, to redemption, and to salvation; while in the sphere of public life he is one, as he says himself, who 'preaches Justice', who 'keeps vigil for the good of the world'. But for the most part, in the *Divine Comedy*, his prophetic office is assumed as a matter of course, rather than expressed in words.

It is in connection with Love—all love, from the crudest to the highest—that he speaks in the most clearly prophetic accents. Nor is this surprising; for Love, as we have seen, is to him the power which moves all things, through their desire for union with God. After thinking for some days about writing in praise of Beatrice, and 'fearing to begin', as he writes in the *Vita Nuova*, 'my tongue spoke as though of its own motion, and said "Ladies who have intelligence of Love"'. Love, says Miss Barclay Carter (*Contemporary Review*, May 1941),

was inspiration in the fullest sense, kindling the heart, enlightening the mind, through a certain divine gift given to poets (his own words). It is the old identification of poet and prophet. 'Do you know, Petrarch once asked, what Dante means by Love in the lines, "who, when love breathes upon me, note"? It is love of the Holy Ghost.' The *Divine Comedy* is to him truly the

> poema sacro
>
> Al quale ha posta mano e cielo e terra,

the sacred song to which both heaven and earth have set their hand (*Par.* XXV, 1, 2).

Milton, on the other hand, thought of God in a far more intimate manner, as revealing himself directly to individuals, imposing on every man his duty, and speaking to him through the Holy Spirit. It is to the Holy Spirit that he prays 'Instruct me, for thou knowest'. His faith that the Spirit will illuminate his darkness, and support his faltering steps, is the deepest of his convictions. His thoughts take poetical shape in his conception of the 'Heavenly Muse'. He is careful to explain that she is not the Muse of Greek mythology who bore that name (Urania): 'The meaning, not the name, I call.'

> Before the hills appeared, or fountain flowed,
> Thou with Eternal Wisdom didst converse,
> Wisdom Thy sister. (*P.L.* vii, 8.)

It is she who inspired Moses, and who loves the hill of Zion and the brook of Siloa. By her he is 'taught to venture down the dark descent, and up to re-ascend'. It is she who 'visits his slumbers nightly, or when Morn purples the East'. She is

> my Celestial Patroness, who deigns
> Her nightly visitation unimplored,
> And dictates to me slumbering, or inspires
> Easy my unpremeditated verse. (*P.L.* ix, 21.)

And when he is haunted by the fear that his great design may fail, because 'an Age too late, or cold climate, or years' may weaken his powers, he adds:

> and much they may, if all be mine,
> Not Hers, who brings it nightly to my ear.
> (*P.L.* ix, 46.)

Milton was a prophet in the sense that he was conscious of a Being by whose inspiration, and on whose behalf, he uttered his message; and his message was that of religion and virtue; he was to exalt the mind of man, and in particular to lead the English people along the path of true civilisation. 'Art is what it is because of what it teaches.'

'These abilities' (those of the poet) 'wheresoever they be found, are the inspired gift of God, rarely bestowed, yet to some in every nation; and are of power, beside the office of a pulpit, to imbreed and cherish in a great people the seeds of virtue and public civility, to allay the perturbations of the mind, and set the affections in the right tune; to celebrate in glorious and lofty hymns the throne and equipage of God's almightiness, and what He works and what He suffers to be wrought with high providence in His church; to sing victorious agonies of martyrs and saints, the deeds and triumphs of just and pious nations, doing valiantly through faith against the enemies of Christ; to deplore the general relapses of kingdoms and states from justice and God's true worship. Lastly, whatsoever in religion is holy and sublime, in virtue amiable or grave, whatsoever hath passion or admiration in all the changes of that which is called fortune from without, or the wily subtleties and reflexes of man's thoughts from within; all these things with a solid and treatable smoothness to paint out and describe.' (From *The Reason of Church Government urged against Prelaty*, 1642, p. 281.)

The great work of art which he contemplates is one which is 'not to be obtained by the invocation of dame memory and her siren daughters, but by devout prayer to that eternal Spirit, who can enrich with all utterance and knowledge, and sends out his seraphim, with the hallowed fire of his altar, to touch and purify the lips of whom he pleases' (*ib.* p. 427).

This high office involves personal consecration.

And long it was not after, when I was confirmed in this opinion, that he who would not be frustrate of his hope to write well hereafter in laudable things, *ought himself to be a true poem*; that is, a composition and pattern of the best and honourablest things; not presuming to sing praises of heroic men, or famous cities, *unless he have in himself* the experience and practice of all that which is praiseworthy.

(From *Apology for Smectymnuus*, 1642, p. 275.)

Goethe's conception of God was much vaguer, and there were frequent fluctuations in the exact form of it. At one time he spoke of God, at another of Nature, at another of God-Nature (*Gott-Natur*). But the constant factor was his belief in the Universe as a divine unity. In *Faust* he speaks dramatically, and therefore not distinctly in his own person. We must therefore look for guidance to what he says elsewhere. 'I believe in God and in Nature, and in the triumph of good over evil', he said to Eckermann (*Conversations*, p. 54), though he could never satisfy the 'pious souls'. Individual men are the mouthpieces of 'Nature'. 'She has neither speech nor language; but she creates hearts and voices, and in them she feels and speaks.' He does, indeed, seem to speak in his own person in the famous speech of Faust in answer to Gretchen's pathetic enquiry as to whether he believes in God (*Faust I*, Martha's Garden). It begins: 'Who dare Him name, or who proclaim, "I believe in Him"? Who would care, or who would dare, to say "I believe not in Him"? The All-embracing, the All-sustaining, embraces and sustains He not, thee, me, Himself?'

> Wer darf ihn nennen?
> Und wer bekennen:
> Ich glaub ihn?
> Wer empfinden
> Und sich unterwinden
> Zu sagen: ich glaub ihn nicht?
> Der Allumfasser,
> Der Allerhalter,
> Fasst und erhalt er nicht
> Dich, mich, sich selbst?

The attitude of Goethe towards his function as poet, though equally far removed from that of the 'pure' artist, differs from those of Virgil, Dante, and Milton. The 'power outside himself' is also a power which operates, to some degree, in all men; the poet could not resist it, even if he wished to do so. What he can do is to make himself more, or less, susceptible to its influence. The distinction between subjectivity and objectivity is the form in which this question suggests itself to Goethe's mind; a distinction very familiar to Germans, though less so to Englishmen. The subjective attitude would lead the artist to look upon himself as standing, as it were, outside the world, and contemplating it; and upon the thoughts and emotions which it inspires in him as being the natural material for poetry. He ought, on the contrary, to look upon himself objectively, as a part of the world and bound up with it; and upon the world as expressing itself through him. He must 'appropriate to himself, and express, the world' (Eckermann, *Conversations*, p. 166). He must be 'susceptible to unusual emotions, and capable of hearing celestial voices' (*ib.* p. 417). 'Art is the true interpreter of the inexpressible' (*Fragment on Nature*). The greatest works of art are a revelation of the ultimate nature of the world and of man. In the beautiful speech of the poet in the *Prologue on the Stage* (*Faust I*), the description begins with Nature and the vast mass of Being; the poet absorbs this and 'consecrates' each detail 'to the whole' (*ruft zur allgemeinen Weihe*). These difficult lines are thus rendered by Van der Smissen, the latest translator in verse, and perhaps the best.

> Who calls each separate chord to general Consecration,
> Where it may throb in glorious unison?

In all this we trace the abiding influence of Spinoza, especially Book v of the *Ethic*, which deals with the 'intellectual love of God' (*amor intellectualis Dei*). Spinoza held that man should strive above all things to break through, and to raise himself above, the interests and the cravings of individuality; to realise the totality of things; to live in the whole. Spinoza was profoundly religious in feeling, but he could only sympathise with organised forms of religion in so far as they helped a man to transcend the limitations of his personal life, and to see things 'in the light of eternity'.

The mode in which this 'power outside himself' enters into the life of man was spoken of by Goethe—it was one of his favourite ideas—as the daemonic, *das Dämonische*. Its operations may be, from the individual's point of view, wholly unconscious. It moves and inspires men to thoughts or actions not consciously intended. It lies behind the greatness of Napoleon and the greatness of Shakespeare. It is, in fact, when it operates powerfully, the thing which distinguishes the great from the insignificant.

> The daemonic is that which cannot be explained by Reason or Understanding; it lies not in my nature, but I am subject to it. . . . In poetry, especially in that which is unconscious, before which reason and understanding fall short, and which therefore produces effects so far surpassing all conception, there is always something daemonic. (*Conversations*, pp. 525, 527.)

Goethe put his finger on a point which is one of the distinctive discoveries of the Modern Age—the part played in all our actions by the unconscious or sub-conscious. Modern psychological research has revealed more clearly what Goethe divined and named the 'daemonic'. It makes, however, no definite assertion as to the ultimate source of the impulses and instincts which it analyses. Freud's followers are applying the newly discovered facts to throw light on the genesis of works of art and literature. The thinker who comes nearest to Goethe's conception is Dr Jung, who goes far beyond his master. Jung develops the idea of the 'collective unconscious'. The unconscious is not merely something belonging to each individual. All men are in touch with it. But in the artist it forms a larger part of his mental being than it does in that of other men.

The very language Jung uses is curiously reminiscent of Goethe's.

'Ideas', he says in *Modern Man in Search of a Soul* (p. 132), 'arise from that realm of procreative, psychic life out of which the ephemeral mind of the single human being grows like a plant, that blossoms, bears fruit and seed, and then withers and dies. Ideas spring from a source which is not contained within one man's personal life. We do not create them; they create us. . . . On the other hand, the subject also is an objective fact, a piece of the world. What issues from it comes, after all, from the universal soil.'

A somewhat similar suggestion was made by F. W. H. Myers in his *Human Personality* long before. Speaking of Socrates, he contends that it is possible that messages 'from the subliminal strata of the personality . . . may sometimes come from far beneath the realm of dream and confusion—from some self whose monitions convey to us a wisdom profounder than we know' (vol. II, p. 95).

The same idea has been suggested, again with regard to Socrates, by Professor J. A. Stewart (*The Myths of Plato*). It is generally supposed that the myths embodied in Plato's *Dialogues* are simply meant to put, as it were, into language intelligible to the masses the philosophy which the rest of the dialogue expresses in logical form, but it is open to question whether they do not represent something more than this. It is suggested that they are really poetry of the highest kind. Socrates (who introduces most of them) speaks so solemnly and impressively, and he introduces matter which goes far beyond what has been indicated in the dialogue. 'He prophesies, and his hearers listen spellbound.'

It may be that some of Goethe's sayings give us the clue to a problem which has been discussed for centuries—what is the essential function of the poet? We are thinking especially of his phrases of a more mystical character—'that which is unconscious, before which Reason and Understanding fall short', 'celestial voices', 'the inexpressible', 'the daemonic'. It may be that the original source of all true poetry is that world of unconsciousness which exists in educated minds as well as in the minds of children and primitive men; which feels, and wills, and acts, but does not reflect; and that the essence of the poet's art consists in revealing, to the hearer or reader, ideas and images from this unconscious region. Such a conclusion would be in harmony with the most modern psychological research.

It may be, to put it briefly, that all true poets are in a sense prophets; that there is, and can be, no such thing as 'pure' poetry in the sense defined at the beginning of this chapter; and that the true poet has, whether he knows it or not, and whether he likes it or not, a prophetic 'mission'.

But we must be aware of committing ourselves too far in this direction. The conclusions reached by Freud and his followers cannot as yet be regarded as established science; the study is still in its infancy. Moreover, even if these conclusions contain an element of truth, there remains a region of thought and feeling in the poet's mind which is as important as ever for the understanding of poetry. This is his conscious mental environment. It is here that the whole form of his poem is determined. Here is the sphere, as Milton puts it, of 'labour and intense study, joined with a strong propensity of nature'. Without this equipment for the necessary effort and shaping, the original source, the spring of inspiration, would remain for ever barren of result; and great, fruitful achievements for mankind, such as the *Aeneid*, the *Divine Comedy*, *Paradise Lost* and *Faust*, would never have come into existence.

Chapter III

THE SIGNIFICANCE OF THE MYTH

Reference has already been made, more than once, to the fact that Virgil, Dante, Milton and Goethe are alike in embodying their wisdom in a 'myth'. This is felt by many modern readers as an obstacle. The narrative form, even the dramatic form in *Faust*, appears too elementary for its purpose, something better adapted to earlier ages and simpler minds than ours. It seems to detract from the seriousness of a work whose purpose is to deal with the profounder issues of life. Is not the importance attributed, in this essay, to such poems as these somewhat of an exaggeration? Are they anything more than striking and finely told stories?

It is true that, on the face of it, the *Aeneid* is merely the story of the Foundation of Rome; the *Divine Comedy* is the story of a journey through Hell, Purgatory, and Paradise; *Paradise Lost* is the story of Adam's Fall; *Faust* is the story of a Renaissance magician who secured the Devil's services to gain Experience, and managed, at the end, to escape paying the Devil's price.

But it is equally clear that these are something more than stories, they are stories of a peculiar kind. First of all, they are associated with a vast range of tradition; and each of them was, before the poet handled it, bound up with many of the deeper thoughts of European man. But more important than this, they direct the mind, with great emphasis, to an unlimited Past in which Man's origins are to be found, and to a Future in the light of which his destiny is interpreted. Finally, in each one an essential part is played by something which is often contemptuously called 'supernatural machinery', but which in fact is the means whereby the human experience described is related to a universal and eternal world. The stories are, in a word, 'cosmic myths'.

That they are stories of a peculiar kind, then, is evident; but that they are, nevertheless, stories, and not formal treatises, does not detract from the seriousness with which they deserve to be studied. It points rather to what is apparently a profound need of human nature.

There may be, as will appear later, more subtle reasons for the 'myth', but one obvious explanation of it lies on the surface. Experience hitherto, at any rate among European peoples, seems to show that any general view of the world, and the practical problem of how to live—if it is to be made real and acceptable to vast masses of men—must be embodied in a series of events, a transaction of some kind, a mythos, or myth, in the Greek sense of the word.

It does not seem that, in the nature of things, this is the only possible form in which such a theme could be presented. It might seem possible to embody it, for example, in the flexible form developed by Hebrew literature, where, as in *Job*, *Isaiah*, or the *Revelation*, a mingling occurs of direct oratory, of dramatic interchange of dialogue, of visions, of lyric song, of choric strophe and antistrophe, of prose and poetry, of repetition and alternation. But, in fact, no one work of this kind has impressed itself on the European mind as have the great poems which embody a 'myth'.

The reference to the Bible brings to mind at once the most significant example of the necessity of the myth. It is to be found, of course, in the great world religions. In each case, the doctrine does not stand alone; it centres round a series of events; and it is the series of events which fixes it in the minds of the great mass of adherents. The Bible is no exception to the rule. It contains a myth, or rather two myths; that which is the foundation of Judaism, and that which is the foundation of Christianity. The first is the history of God's dealings with the Chosen People. The second, which takes the first as the prediction and type of things to come, is the history of the Life, the Death, and the Resurrection of Christ.

To call these histories 'myths' is not to pronounce any judgment for or against their historical accuracy. We must rid our minds of the disparaging associations which have gathered round the word in modern times. The myth is not something 'mythical'. By a 'myth' the Greeks meant simply a story. 'Mythology' was simply 'story-telling'. In the present connection, attention is merely called to its use as a fact of experience. All the great religions are quoted merely as examples of a necessity which lies deep in human nature.

It is, therefore, no matter for surprise that any writer who aims at a wide popular appeal must use a myth as the vehicle for his thoughts. Dante and Milton adopt the established myths of religion. Virgil and Goethe select theirs from the incidents of human history handed down to us by long tradition.

To the Englishman, a convincing illustration of this fact will be found in a book which, for at least a century, was the most widely popular, next to the Bible, of all English books—the *Pilgrim's Progress* of John Bunyan. Bunyan, when he wished to bring home the Puritan theology to the English people, told them the immortal tale of a pilgrim's progress from the City of Destruction to the Celestial City. His title itself is highly suggestive. It might be applied to Aeneas in his wanderings, to Dante in his divinely guided journey, or to Faust in his cycle of experience.

An example which is even more significant, from the point of view of this essay, may be drawn from our own time. It is one to which reference has already been made—Hardy's *Dynasts*. In that colossal epic drama, or dramatic epic (the poet uses both terms), Hardy expresses his conception of life by telling the story of the chief crisis (from the British point of view) in the Napoleonic Wars. But he does not tell the story merely as it appears to the historian. He introduces 'supernatural machinery'—a Chorus of Spirits—the Ancient Spirit of the Years, the Spirit of the Pities, the Spirit Ironic, Recording Angels, and so forth—not because he believes in them—he was the last man from whom we should expect 'supernaturalism'—but because, as he tells us, he felt it necessary to create some means whereby 'a modern outlook' on the whole story might be expressed. The Spirits relate the story to the general scheme of things, to the 'modern outlook'—even though the poet does not set forth any 'clear metaphysic' or 'systematised philosophy'. He was content that the Spirits should be recognised as deliberate inventions, provided he could make them real enough to command 'poetic faith'—which Coleridge defines as 'the willing suspension of disbelief' on the part of the reader. In other words, 'supernatural machinery' appeared to Hardy, as much as to the Christian Milton, to be essential for his purpose.

A final illustration of the inevitableness of the myth may be drawn from a very different sphere—that of contemporary politics. The two great doctrines, or fanaticisms as some would call them, which at the time this book was written were capturing the minds of the youth of Europe, are Communism and National Socialism. Though primarily political doctrines, they both aspire to provide an outlook on the world in general—to be, in the jargon of to-day, 'ideologies'. They are indeed, as Mr Voigt points out in his admirable study *Unto Caesar*, 'secular religions'. To propagate its view of things, each maintains an elaborate system of education; and in order to make this education effective, the beginner is invariably instructed, at the outset, in a definite account of world history. This account is, in fact, the myth required. Each of these secular religions has found in practice that, without such a myth, widespread success would be impossible.

The Germans, self-conscious as always in their thinking, explicitly recognise the need; while the doctrine is embodied in *Mein Kampf*, the text-book of National Socialism is Alfred Rosenberg's *Myth of the Twentieth Century (Der Mythus des 20. Jahrhunderts)* which has been placed in the library of every school. The writer is a commonplace charlatan, it is true; but none the less, the glorification of his book by the State is a proof of the importance of the National Socialist myth, which may be baldly summarised as follows: 'In the beginning, God created Races; the Aryan Race was destined to lead the world in culture; the Nordic branch in particular, in which God specially reveals himself.'

Nor can there be any question as to what is the myth of Communism; it is the Marxian interpretation of history. 'In the beginning there were economic conditions. Their changes, traceable all through Man's history, have moulded his mind, and therefore his institutions. This process is continuing now. Man is capable of attaining material prosperity and social peace. The culmination will be reached when, all over the Earth, the expropriators are expropriated, and the Union of Republics is complete.' That is the Apocalypse; more may yet be revealed, but beyond this culmination the Marxist myth does not, as yet, lift the curtain of futurity.

What is not quite so easy to understand is that the concrete forms of the myth—the simple statements, the living personalities, the movements, the events—have an attraction, not merely for the simple minds, but also for the more

sophisticated. The man whose activity is mainly intellectual instinctively turns to them as providing something
more than the formal treatise. He may be well able to
grasp an abstract conception intellectually, without the
aid of a story; but he still feels in himself a strong tendency
to see that conception as the poets have represented it,
embodied in one or other of those actions or persons which
the great works of art have made familiar to him. The
writer of a treatise on ethics, for example, finds it hard to
resist giving point to his argument by a quotation or allusion to some great poem. It is one thing to know that there
are moments when 'we feel that we are greater than we
know'; it is another thing to recall the speech of Ulysses
to his friends in Dante's narrative: 'Consider your origin;
ye were not formed to live like brute-beasts, but to follow
after Virtue and Knowledge.'

> Considerate la vostra semenza;
> Fatti non foste a viver come bruti,
> Ma per seguir virtute e conoscenza.
>
> (*Inf.* xxvi, 118.)

It is one thing to know the paralysing effect of worry and
fussiness upon the practical life; it is another thing to see
it incorporated in the spectral figure of Care (*Sorge*)—
Faust's last enemy, who can strike him blind, but whom
even in his blindness he learns how to defy. It is one thing
to be able to define a moral ideal—say that of fortitude—
in one's scheme of ethics; it is another thing to dwell upon
Milton's conception of Abdiel, alone and confronting the
rebel angels,

> Unshaken, unseduced, unterrified;

or Farinata's glance of unconquerable scorn, 'as though
he held Hell itself in great contempt'—

> Come avesse lo Inferno in gran dispitto.

The fact is that the more we think of the universal appeal of the myth—or at any rate of the cosmic myth, which purports to give an account of the universe—the more we doubt whether the obvious explanation hitherto given is not too simple and superficial to meet the case.

This doubt was suggested to me by reading Professor J. A. Stewart's exhaustive study, *The Myths of Plato*. Plato's practice—he introduces myths into no less than nine of his dialogues—is instructive. We generally suppose that the philosopher, having completed his argument, and fully met the needs of his philosophic students, then proceeds to embody his conclusion in a picturesque story, to bring it home to the multitude, as John Bunyan did in his *Pilgrim's Progress*. But when we turn to the myth itself, we find that it contains a great deal more than has been developed in the argument; that it is in itself a complete and striking work of art; that it is introduced and presented with great solemnity; that it seems to be a new way of approaching fundamental truths; not a mere translation of the argument into popular terms, but rather a distinct method of describing things as they are. The words put into the mouth of Socrates, speaking of the myth in the *Phaedo*, which deals with the fate of souls after death, are significant.

> The moral of the whole story, Simmias, is this: that we should do all that we can to partake of Virtue and Wisdom, in this life. . . . Not that I insist upon all the particulars of my tale—no sensible man would; but that it, or something like it, is true concerning our souls and their mansions after death— since we are agreed that the soul is immortal—this, it seems to me, is a proper opinion, and enough to justify some venture of imagination in a believer. . . . It is right to relate such things, and to chant them over to oneself. (*Phaedo*, 114.)

The reference to 'chanting' is inserted because the Greek expression (ἐπᾴδειν ἑαυτῷ—literally, 'sing over oneself') is one that is used of repeating charms. The idea is worth noting. We are, we might say, to 'dwell upon' the myth—to employ an expression so often used in the writings of the 'New Thought' and similar modern developments of religious speculation.

The words which Plato here puts into the mouth of Socrates suggest that the myth is something more than a 'popularisation'. Socrates, we know, was interested almost exclusively in the problem of 'how to live'—in ethics. It has been suggested that, in his opinion, metaphysical questions could not be profitably discussed at all—except in the form of myths—and that the myth was a regular feature of his philosophic conversations.

The myth appeals primarily to that original part of the mind which sees but does not think, or only thinks collectively with the tribe of which the individual is a member; and which is, perhaps, the whole of primitive man's mind. Hence his universal love of story-telling. Art, we may say, is to him his language. He has no other. A poetic story—a primitive piece of drama—a statue or a building—these are the means whereby he expresses the whole of what he apprehends of the world around him.

But this original, primordial part of the mind has still its place in our psychical inheritance, side by side with the thinking or reasoning element. We may illustrate the point by referring to the religious consciousness of civilised men. Does it make no difference, let us ask, to the consciousness of the Christian that his conception of the divine government of the Universe is embodied in a record of events—a mythos, in the Greek sense of the word? Again I insert the caution that in using the word 'mythos' I am not pronouncing against the truth of the events recorded in the Christian gospel; I am referring merely to the fact that they take the form of concrete actions and words—of events in time. Would it be the same thing to the philosophically educated Christian to appreciate in the abstract that God's purpose is to 'save' mankind, and that the interest of all humanity is to cóoperate as one whole with that purpose, as it is to accept the fact that God became incarnate, at a certain time, in a human personality— who said, among many other things, 'Inasmuch as ye have done it unto one of the least of these my brethren, ye have done it unto me'?

The answer of orthodox Christians, I think, if they were to faċe this question, would be an emphatic negative. It would *not* be the same thing. The events themselves are of the essence. The vivid, concrete embodiment of the bare doctrine—the element of incarnation—not merely makes an appeal to the emotional side of man's nature, but brings him nearer to the absolute truth of things as they are.

We may go further. The mystic, in all religions, is distinguished from the rationalist by the fact that he does not infer and conclude, step by step; he 'sees' things in concrete and definite shape, as a whole, by one single process. Seeing, contemplating—intuition, not ratiocination—is the note of mysticism, in every one of its many forms.

Wordsworth tells us how, in that 'serene and blessed mood' which comes from the loving contemplation of nature,

> We are laid asleep
> In body, and become a living soul;
> While with an eye made quiet by the power
> Of harmony, and the deep power of joy,
> We see into the life of things.

In the *Revelation*, it is always 'I saw seven golden candlesticks' or 'I saw a new heaven and a new earth'. Dante, following St Thomas Aquinas, distinguishes between the knowledge which he obtained by Human Reason, and that which he obtained by direct Revelation; in his *Paradiso*, the whole emphasis is on light, on vision.

So too, Faust has his vision (Part II, Act I) of a mysterious land, outside space and time, where reign 'The Mothers' (*die Mütter*); and he who would bring Absolute Beauty (personified in Helen) into the common ways of men must first visit this land—the home of the ultimate ideas or realities.

The classic description of the mystical experience may be found in the final canto of Dante's *Paradiso*—that canto which, taken in its colossal context, represents perhaps the highest flight to which poetic speech has ever attained. Dante there tells how his sight became purged (*la mia vista venendo sincera*)- and was mightier than language (*fu maggio che 'l parlar nostro*). He was as one who has dreamed, when the intense feeling stamped upon him remains, but naught else comes back to the mind:

> la passione impressa
> Rimane, e l' altro alla mente non riede.

He gazed upon the Eternal Light, and there, he says, 'I saw ingathered, bound by Love in one volume, the scattered leaves of all the Universe':

> Nel suo profondo vidi, che s' interna
> Legato con Amore in un volume,
> Ciò che per l' Universo si squaderna.

And he goes on to say, in one of his brief but pregnant similes drawn from psychology, that the memory of what he actually saw is more completely blotted out than is mankind's memory of the voyage of the Argonauts, twenty-five centuries ago. Yet he prays that he may be empowered to record something—'be it but a single spark'—of the glory that he saw; and he tells us that he saw three circles (the Trinity) and that, in some way which he cannot explain, the colour of the second circle

(Christ) was painted with 'our image' (*nostra effige*)—the human face.

There is, then, a part of the mind which sees realities, or what it deems realities, by the direct method of intuition. And it may be that, to this part of the mind, the cosmic myth, presented by the mysterious power of the poet's imagination, pictures certain truths about the Universe as a whole, which are beyond the reach of the rational process; that it can bring us nearer to reality, not only giving us a 'feeling' that we see the real world, but enabling us actually to see that world in a new aspect. The thought is at least worth suggesting. Without pretending to deal adequately with the metaphysical problems of reality and the possibility of knowledge, one may at least hazard the speculation that Reason can pronounce on any part of the universe, but not on the whole. Reason cannot, as it were, get outside the whole—outside the totality of things, including its own operations. But the poet's imagination can; it gives us access, albeit fitfully and vaguely, to a 'transcendent' sphere of knowledge. The myth becomes, in the hands of one more gifted and more alive than we are, a 'vision' of real things.

This is a suggestion rather than a conclusion. What is certain is that the poet's imagination gives him the power to move more boldly and freely than the logician. It leaps forward to the conclusion in a flash—or by a process so rapid that it seems like a flash. It is not on its guard, at each moment, against the assaults of the critical intellect. It need not wait to verify each step before it takes the next one. It can assert things without being irrevocably committed to them; and it can then see them in the light of their relation to the whole. If it instinctively creates a picture, or a musical structure, that is because it feels the inevitable feebleness of language; there is so much to be expressed which cannot be expressed in logical terms.

All we can say on this obscure subject is that, if there is any truth in the thought here tentatively put forward, then it becomes doubly easy to understand why Virgil, Dante, Milton and Goethe, in their different ways, presented their conceptions of the universe under the form and similitude of a myth. The particular mode in which each of them handled his myth will be the subject of the next chapter.

Chapter IV

THE POET'S USE OF THE MYTH

I. *The kind of myth preferred by the poet-prophet*

We have discussed the reasons why any broad conception of life is so often expressed in a 'myth', whether by
the poet, the prophet, or even the political 'ideologist'.
The way has been prepared for the consideration of our
four poets in this matter of the myth. It is both interesting
and fruitful to see what kind or type of myth has been
shown by experience to suit the purpose of a 'poet-
prophet'.

Judging by the practice of these poets, it would seem
that certain elements are essential. There must be a central
figure who passes through a series of experiences. This
central figure need not be, as the rules of 'epic' poetry
were thought to require, a man of exalted rank, fame, or
distinction; but he must be one who is sufficiently 'human'
to be imagined as representative of mankind in its strivings
and failures. Such are Aeneas—Dante himself—Adam—
Faust. It is perhaps the one inherent weakness of Milton's
myth that Adam, in his perfect innocence and ignorance
of evil before the Fall, is a figure so remote from all our
experience that it is well-nigh impossible to invest him
with real interest.

This central figure must be in some sort of relation to
the world of eternal realities, independent of the fluctuations of human life and the supposed 'interests' of the
world of time. Hence what is known as the 'supernatural
machinery' of all four myths. Hitherto, at any rate, this
has been found essential; we have no example of a poet-
prophet whose conception was one of 'pure' agnosticism;

as we have seen in the last chapter, not even Hardy could dispense with 'supernatural machinery' in his epic drama of *The Dynasts*.

Another common element is that none of the four poets constructs a myth of his own. This was the method of Plato, but it is not theirs. Plato's use of the myth is highly suggestive. He was unquestionably a poet in all but name. But he was primarily a philosopher; and though he drew largely on traditional material, especially on the Orphic writings and rituals relating to the future life, his purpose required him to subordinate this material rather strictly to the philosophic view or attitude which he aimed at inculcating; thus the main structure of the myth is his own.

The method of the poet-prophet is different. He aims at a much wider immediate appeal; an appeal to the mass of men, the uneducated as well as the cultured. He has undertaken a task of stupendous difficulty; he cannot afford to add to it by embarking on the further task of familiarising his 'public' with a wholly new myth. He takes full advantage of what already exists in their minds. He singles out a myth round which a whole world of tradition has already gathered. He begins by assuming that the outline of his story is already familiar to most of his hearers or readers.

Part of the effort of imagination which the modern reader must make is to put himself in the position of those first hearers or readers. To him the story may be new; but he must contrive to read the poem as if the story were already part of his mental furniture; he must not expect the poet to use all the arts of exposition which the modern novelist uses to bring home his narrative to the mind. He must make himself, to some extent, like the Roman or Italian citizen who had learned at his mother's knee of Alba Longa and Romulus, the Decii and the Scipios, the priest of Nemi, the shrines of Picus and Faunus. Or again—an easier task—he must feel something of the tense atmosphere of passionate religious and political controversy in mid-seventeenth-century England; he must feel the English Bible to be a new book, with all the freshness and impressiveness of what our modern slang calls a 'best seller'. He must realise the wild hopes and dreams of the Cromwellian interlude, and the crash of counter-revolution in 1660.

These conditions are essential, it seems, from the point of view of those to whom the poem is addressed. But there are at least two other conditions which still further limit the poet's choice. These are essential from the point of view of the poet himself.

The first is that the myth should be capable of forming a basis for the illustration of the great theme. It must be, if not already adapted, at least easily adaptable, to this purpose. It must be one which can readily be 'generalised' so as to bear the weight of the poet's reflections on human life as a whole.

Clearly, for this purpose, the story must be rich in characters, in incidents, in changes of fortune. It would be too narrow, for instance, if it were a series of a man's unconnected adventures like the *Odyssey*, or merely told the progress of a great conqueror from humble beginnings to supreme power. Variety is needed to provide opportunities for trial, for choice, for error; and more generally, to leave in the mind a profound impression of the complexity and multiplicity of human events.

And the story must be on the grand scale; it must concern great numbers of men; trivial events might indeed be allegorised, but the spirit, the atmosphere, of a serious and comprehensive conception would be lost. The scope of the story, the background of the picture, must be large; in each of the four poets, the scope extends from the first plans of Providence to some culmination in the world of eternity. Milton's scope is the greatest, for it alone extends, not only to all space, but to all time—from the original chaos out of which the world was created to the final restitution of all things. Yet Dante's is perhaps the most perfectly suited to his purpose. If at first sight it is confined to the 'other world', he has given to the narrative a character of full and vivid humanity; partly by making it, in one aspect, an allegory of human life—we have his own authority for this; partly by his conception of the 'Earthly Paradise' as the realisation of all purely human strivings, unaided by Revelation; partly by his independent treatment of Hell, Purgatory and Paradise; and above all by the vast variety of human stories and historical events, introduced incidentally.

The second condition which is certainly essential, from the poet's point of view, is that his myth must be one upon which his imagination can seize with spiritual and intellectual ardour. While its literal truth or untruth is, as we shall see, a secondary consideration, it remains a fact that the poet must be near enough in sympathy to those who believe or believed in it to make it real for imaginative purposes. It must not be dry and lifeless, a mere mechanical device. He must be able to exercise his powers upon it with ease and joy and freedom.

II. *Did these poets consciously choose their myths to illustrate their view of life?*

From the point of view adopted in this essay, the main interest centres upon the conception of life conveyed by each poem. But it by no means follows that the poet began, in point of time, with this conception of life, and then consciously chose a myth in which to embody it and commend it to the world. On the contrary, the myth was generally chosen as a good subject for narrative or drama, without any such definite intention or purpose; it was only at a later stage, as experience was accumulated and thought was developed, that it rose to a unique position in the poet's mind, and became recognised as a fit vehicle for his ripest wisdom and his highest ideals.

Such, at least, was generally the case so far as the poet's consciousness was concerned. Whether, in his unconscious mind, another process was at work is a question too difficult to answer in our present state of knowledge; it is at least possible that a secret urge to express his deepest thought, to see things whole and to embody the vision in a single work of art, was always present, and that this secret urge in fact determined the choice of the myth. Decisions vital from the artistic point of view are undoubtedly taken in ways which the artist himself cannot account for. Goethe was keenly conscious of this fact, as has been pointed out already in connection with the use of the term 'prophet'.

The first nucleus of each poem has already been described in chapter I, in order to show how in every case the great poem, as it issued ultimately from the crucible of the poet's imagination, was present to his mind in embryo from his early years. It became, in the end, the main work of his life. Here it is only necessary, without repeating the details, to point out that the first nucleus was not originally chosen to embody the poet's whole conception of life. Gradually, he realised that it was well fitted for this wider purpose. The first nucleus was chosen for its own sake, and was something narrower and more limited than the thing to which it finally grew.

Thus Virgil's first thought was to honour and gratify Augustus by producing a poem on the Emperor's achievements—the conquests in Egypt, in Asia Minor, in Armenia, in Parthia—and on his ancestors beginning with the mythical kings of Troy, themselves descended from

Jupiter—'father Tros' and Assaracus. These points are indicated in a passage in his *Georgics* (iii, 8–48), to which reference has already been made. It may date from about 37 B.C., whereas the *Aeneid* was not begun till 29 B.C.

It is very significant, however, that even at that early date this subject is associated with a Descent to the World of the Dead. It may well have been that Virgil had some idea, even then, of representing Augustus as summing up in his person, as it were, the whole majestic history of the Foundation of Rome—as the poet afterwards did in the speech of Anchises to his son, with which the scenes in Hades culminate in the Sixth Book of the *Aeneid*.

Gradually, we may conjecture, this fruitful idea, as it germinated in the poet's mind, came to be the very central point of his story. He found that the theme thus sketched in early manhood was well adapted to carry the weight of all his human ideals, and of those philosophic speculations, those 'dearer studies' (*potiora studia*) to which, as his biographer tells us, he would fain have devoted his life.

In other words, the poem was first conceived as one of the biographical type—like the numerous Achilleids, Heracleids, and so forth, which were then a popular form of literature. This type, however, Virgil definitely rejected. The central thought of the *Aeneid* became something very different—the birth of a great people, with a message and a function for all mankind. The story could convey what we might call his philosophy of history—the slow upward growth of civilisation through Man's labour and suffering and sorrow, in loyal obedience to divine guidance. Meanwhile, probably during the composition of the *Georgics*, his philosophical outlook had changed from the Epicurean to the Stoic. The change involved a world of difference. Epicurus had denied all planned operation of Providence. Virgil now saw the political world at close quarters, having been taken into the intimate circle of Augustus and

Maecenas. He became convinced that a Divine Power had guided Rome from the chaos of the Civil Wars to the order and peace established by the Emperor. It was a change from negation to affirmation, and it carried with it a solemn sense of responsibility.

Dante, again, thought first of a poem much more limited in scope than the *Divine Comedy*, though sufficient in itself to tax his highest powers. In 1290, after the death of Beatrice Portinari, he thought of describing, no doubt in some extended form, his vision of Beatrice in Paradise, described in the words quoted in chapter 1. But great changes took place in his life during the next ten years. About 1295, at the age of thirty, he began, for the first time, to study philosophy seriously. He mastered the greater part of the knowledge of his time. What was even more important, he entered about the same time into politics. In 1300 he was elected as one of the six 'Priors', the highest office under the Florentine constitution of that time. Boccaccio, appointed fifty years after the poet's death to a professorial chair to lecture on the *Divine Comedy*, tells us definitely that it was his political life which caused his choice of subject. 'Dante looked down from the high places of the Government of the Commonwealth of Florence, wherein he was stationed, and observed over a wide prospect such as is visible from such elevated places, what was the life of men, and what the errors of the common herd.' He saw life in three essentially different forms—the life of vice, the life which abandons vice and makes for virtue, and the life of virtue itself. 'After long meditation beforehand upon what he should write', continues Boccaccio, he began the poem on which he 'continually laboured' till his death in 1321.

We see that the poem has by this time assumed an altogether new form. Beatrice, instead of appearing first in Paradise, descends into Hell in order to commission

Virgil to be Dante's guide through Hell and Purgatory. The whole of Hell, Purgatory and Paradise is to be the scope of the poem. Before he was exiled from Florence in 1302, he had written the first seven cantos of the *Inferno*. He supposed these to have been lost, but when they were brought to him in 1306 in the Lunigiana, he was persuaded by his host Malaspina to resume the great work. The *Inferno* was not finished till 1319, but by then the *Purgatorio* had been begun, and was finished about the same year. Meantime, but not till 1316, the *Paradiso*—the realisation of the youthful vision—had been begun, and occupied the rest of his life; roughly, the period of relative comfort and prosperity which he passed at Ravenna, as the guest of Guido da Polenta. It may well have been that the full import of the work was not realised by him till 1318, when he wrote out his thoughts upon its meanings, literal and allegorical, in the famous *Epistle to Can Grande*—the intimate and discerning patron to whom he submitted each instalment of the poem as it was written.

Of all the four poets, it is Milton who comes nearest to a conscious and deliberate choice. We have seen that, in his early Latin poems, he appears as contemplating a great national epic or drama, based on the Arthurian cycle of legends. But by 1641, as we see from the lists preserved in the library of Trinity College, Cambridge, he had turned over in his mind a very large number of other possible subjects, some of them worked out in detail. He lays great stress on his choice of subject, and in *Paradise Lost* (Book IX) he describes himself as 'long choosing, and beginning late'.

At what stage the Arthurian legend was abandoned, and the vastly greater theme adopted, is unfortunately a question we cannot determine. It involved the complete supersession of a national ideal in favour of a human ideal. And it involved an infinitely greater scope. The Loss of

Paradise had already figured (in 1641) among the subjects which Milton was pondering, and had indeed been worked out in more detail than most. But it is likely that the change did not occur until his greatest political activity was passed, and his blindness recognised (about 1652) as final and incurable. As William Watson wrote:

> He gave thee back Original Night, his own
> Tremendous canvas, large and blank and free,
> Where at each thought a star flashed out and sang.

As for Goethe, it is certain that, even if it had not become his life's work, a drama on Dr Faustus would have been one of his most precious legacies. The story fascinated him from boyhood; but the idea of making Faust the representative of Humanity was only present in a vague form at the outset. The *Urfaust*, written about 1775, in his twenty-sixth year, shows what this drama would have been. There was no *Prologue in Heaven*; no experience of the wider world, with its manifold problems, to complete the single, terrible episode of the scholar's degradation; the last words are the despairing cry of Gretchen from the prison. And there was no culmination in Heaven. The import of these essential changes was not made known to the world till the publication of the completed First Part in 1808.

III. *Must these poets believe in their myths?*

The degree in which Virgil, Dante, Milton and Goethe 'believe in' their myths, in the sense in which the modern man uses the word 'believe', is a question of extraordinary human interest. It is generally the question which occurs first to the English reader. It is one, however, of great subtlety, and can only be considered usefully in each case separately.

Virgil, in all probability, was quite indifferent to the historical truth of his story, and did not 'believe in' the separate gods as spiritual beings, though Venus and Juno represent the special or particular 'fates' of Troy and Greece. But he would have said that 'Jupiter' was the symbol of the power which rules the Universe, and had in it, like the Christian God, the element of personality. Behind Jupiter, however, is Fate—the necessity of things. When Aeneas concludes the long recital of his wanderings before the throng of eager listeners in Dido's palace, the poet's brief summary is 'Thus did he recount the story of his travels, the story of his divine destiny'—

Fata renarrabat divom cursusque docebat.

Virgil is so essentially like ourselves that it does not seem difficult—once one has steeped oneself in his poetry—to speak with some degree of confidence as to his 'beliefs'. With Dante the case is very different. Here we are in touch with a world of thought which, though thirteen centuries nearer in time, is yet far more remote in spirit from our own. If we were to judge by Dante's treatment of Pagan philosophy, or contemporary science—of history, or art, or nature, or by the complete and sovereign independence with which he handles the merit or demerit of this or that person—we should say that his intellect, perhaps the most piercing ever granted to the sons of men, moved with absolute freedom. Yet this same Dante says himself that he implicitly accepts every word that Holy Church teaches, and we have no reason to doubt his honesty. How far he meant to go beyond the actual decisions of General Councils and the solemn declarations of certain Popes—mainly on the Nature of God, the Trinity, the Incarnation, the Catholic Church—we cannot say. He seems to accept, further, the general outlines of the vast popular structure of belief, though here a wide freedom of interpretation was allowed. The Earth is the centre of the Universe, Hell in its bowels, Purgatory on its surface, Paradise in the Empyrean, outside the vast globe of the revolving spheres. Boccaccio tells the story that Dante wrote out in verse his whole creed, in a manner which completely satisfied an Inquisitor who had suspected him of heresy.

We are tempted to ask, did this 'acceptance' really mean 'belief' at all, in the sense in which we use the word? Or did it mean a mere expression of loyalty, a tacit decision not to apply the questioning intellect to a certain defined sphere of thought? But again, could Dante make this distinction between belief and doubt; could he put such a question to himself at all? Virgil, we feel, if he did not in fact put it, could well have done so. But could Dante?

We moderns put it as a matter of course; we draw the distinction between real belief or conviction on the one hand, and the various stages of doubt on the other, because it is a part of the whole background of our thought. Perhaps we do not realise the full revolutionary character of those wonderful *Meditations* of Descartes, the founder of modern philosophy, where he tells us how he solemnly resolved to doubt, with absolute sincerity, everything of which he was not really convinced. Could anyone, before Descartes, draw the distinction—any European at least, since the night of the Dark Ages settled down?

However this may be, Dante's acceptance of the Church's teaching did not prevent him from moving with complete independence outside a very narrowly defined sphere of doctrine. He generally followed precisely the great systematisation of Catholic thought made by St Thomas Aquinas, as did other men of his day. But even here, he felt himself at liberty, outside certain clear limits, to re-interpret in a different way from Aquinas. The punishments of Hell are not the mere penal consequences of past sin; they are what men inevitably suffer who never turn away from the evil motive and the evil desire. Hell is in this world—not in the future life alone. Each sin brings its appropriate judgment on itself. Dante's Hell is the demonstration of the essential awfulness of sin. The description of Purgatory, again, is original. The souls there turn wholly away from the evil and towards the good; and when they are purged, they find themselves in the Earthly Paradise, the original Garden of Eden; in other words, they have reached the stage of human perfection reached by Adam, a stage which is as much a part of God's scheme of redemption as is the further stage of transcendental revelation, realised in Paradise. Again, he makes Eunoe, the river of Happy Thought—apparently his own invention—flow by the side of Lethe, the traditional river of Forgetfulness.

Even Paradise itself is not quite the final and static condition described by Aquinas; the souls still appear to Dante in the various spheres appropriate to each; and are still concerned with this world of ours, though their final seat and resting-place is in the Empyrean, where the Church Triumphant contemplates and adores.

Quite apart from all these independent interpretations, he makes the literal story, as he tells us in his *Epistle to Can Grande*, wholly allegorical. Here we come to Dante's real, at any rate to his intense beliefs. The poem is designed to set forth two meanings above and beyond itself. The first is the course of Man's life here on Earth. 'The subject is Man,' he says, 'liable to the reward or punishment of justice, according as, through the freedom of the will, he is deserving or undeserving.' The second is the 'anagogic' or 'upward-leading' meaning—the conversion from sin to the state of grace, and the 'exitus' or escape of the soul from the bondage of the life here on Earth to the liberty of eternal glory; the object is to guide those living in this life 'to a state of happiness'.

Milton's is the case in which we can form the clearest idea of the attitude adopted; for the evidence is ample. His treatise *De Doctrina Christiana* (which only came to light at the beginning of the nineteenth century) gives us a very full account of the Protestant theology as he saw it. It was compiled with infinite care and reflection, at different periods of his life. We do not find the note of conviction, however, equally present in every page. The book was designed to be a systematic account of the true Protestant faith based entirely on the words of the Bible. It was intended to guide large masses of men in other countries besides his own; it was written in Latin, an infallible sign that he was appealing to an international audience. Theologians know well the subtle distinction between what is intensely and personally appreciated by the writer, and on the other hand what he deems to be the right thing for men in general to believe, what is consistent and comprehensive as part of a system, and what is assimilated most readily. Milton's real convictions fluctuated from time to time, as is well known; and such fluctuations cannot be reflected in a systematic treatise of this kind. To find the note of real conviction, we shall do well to form our impressions from less guarded utterances, utterances that obviously spring from a full heart, such as are to be found in the poems, and in many illuminating passages of his prose works. If *Paradise Lost* be carefully read, the reader will feel that Milton's beliefs at that time, held intensely and intimately, are not very difficult to discern and define. Evidently the Bible is the supreme authority; but each man has the solemn responsibility of interpreting it for himself, in the light of God's revelation in his heart. Clearly there is a place here for the human reason, linking the Christian conception to the creed of the ancient Stoics. For the human reason is itself something divine. It is the direct gift of God, and God does not mean it to rust unused.

In carefully chosen words, he tells us that God's truths are
> Left only in those written records pure—
> Though not but by the spirit understood.

(1) *The Fall of Man.* This was an event in time—the dreadful mysterious origin of all Evil in the world. Milton faced the difficulty of understanding it, for Man in his innocence, Man in God's image, can have had no evil disposition. He attributes it—strange as it may seem at first sight—to mere frivolity, to the want of a sense of responsibility, and light-hearted disobedience to God's commands.

(2) *The Atonement.* This is never the mere death of Christ as an expiation. It is His death as the supreme expression of obedience, fortitude, and burning love. Love is the real redeeming power—Christ is

> By merit, more than birthright, Son of God.

God exalts Him

> because in Thee
> Love hath abounded, more than glory abounds.

And Michael, foretelling the coming of Christ, says of Him:

> The Law of God exact he shall fulfil
> Both by Obedience and by Love, though Love
> Alone fulfil the Law.   (*P. L.* xii, 402.)

Milton was accused in his day, and with some justice, of 'Arianism', or Unitarianism. In the *De Doctrina Christiana* the most notable feature is the immense pains devoted to showing that Christ, though divine, was not 'consubstantial' with the Father. If he had used modern language, Milton would assuredly have said that Trinitarianism robbed Jesus of Nazareth of His intense humanity.

'Arminianism' was the term most used in his day for this Unitarian tendency; it was regarded by the Presbyterians as heretical, on the ground that it belittled, if it did not actually deny, the divinity of Christ; and also that it asserted, as against Calvin, the Freedom of Man's Will. Again and again, in *Paradise Lost*, Milton insists on the fundamental character of Free Will. It should be added that he was for some time a member, like Cromwell, of the sect of the Independents; and that he had considerable sympathy with the central idea of Quakerism—variously described by the founders as the Seed, the True Light, 'that of God' in Man, Christ in the heart.

(3) *The Holy Spirit.* Milton, in later life, never regarded Him as an equal person of the Trinity; yet the belief in Him was fundamental. He is an inbreathing and guiding power, through whom God speaks directly, without the mediation of priest or presbyter, to the heart and mind of the individual man.

> So much the rather thou, Celestial Light,
> Shine inward, and the mind through all her powers
> Irradiate.
>
> (*P.L.* III, 51.)

Reference has already been made (chapter II) to the vivid personification of the 'Heavenly Muse'.

Apart from these beliefs, it seems that the whole story of *Paradise Lost* was regarded by Milton as symbolical. Satan, the Rebel Angels, Abdiel, Raphael, Michael, the beauty of the Garden of Eden, the fatal apple, the expulsion by the Flaming Cherubim, with all the innumerable details surrounding them, were shadows of things deeper and more spiritual. In his long dialogue with Adam, occupying the greater part of three books, the Archangel Raphael tells him

> Of things above his world, and of their being
> Who dwell in Heaven.
>
> (*P.L.* V, 455.)

These spiritual realities Milton 'converts to proper substance', to make them intelligible to 'human sense'. And here he introduces a passage which has great significance for the whole poem.

> and what surmounts the reach
> Of human sense, I shall delineate so,
> By likening spiritual to corporal forms,
> As may express them best; though what if Earth
> Be but the shadow of Heaven, and things therein
> Each to other like, more than on Earth is thought?
>
> (*P.L.* v, 571.)

The suggestion is that 'things therein'—i.e. things in Heaven and things on earth—may have a real resemblance, and not only a symbolised one. The 'shadow' metaphor expresses, not the unsubstantial character of the shadow, but its correspondence with the spiritual truth. Isaac Pennington, one of the pioneers of Quakerism, had the same idea when he wrote: 'All truth is a shadow except the last—except the utmost. Yet every truth is true in its kind...the shadow is a true shadow, as the substance is a true substance.'

With Goethe, we return to a myth that resembles Virgil's, inasmuch as, unlike Dante's and Milton's, it is not itself primarily an expression of certain theological doctrines, but is a story drawn from the ordinary secular life of men. And again, the intellectual background and atmosphere resemble those of Virgil's age. The problem is therefore a much simpler one, and can be treated more shortly. Goethe believed in the slender historical basis of the story of Dr Faustus, the sixteenth-century magician. He was indeed attracted by the story ever since, as a mere boy, he saw it represented in a puppet-show. His original *Faust*, or *Urfaust*, probably begun in his twenty-sixth year, shows an intense interest in the various traditional incidents such as the confusion of the rollicking, tippling students by Mephistopheles' magical creation of all the best wines, followed by a mysterious conflagration. He altered the story, however, beyond recognition; he soon became completely indifferent to its truth or untruth, and treated it deliberately as a vehicle for expressing his deepest thoughts and experiences. Indeed, the conception of the Second Part, in which Faust becomes typical of human life in all its manifold relationships, was present with him, as he said to Eckermann in 1825, almost from the first years of composition. The underlying truths, in which he really believed, were those already referred to in chapter II and others which will be discussed below in chapter VII. It was these which his imagination gradually shaped into imperishable forms through the outward events of the drama.

The essential difference between his myth and that of Virgil is one which is profoundly suggestive. Virgil's imagination treats his Aeneas as the embodiment of a great people and a great state—the 'Senate and People of Rome', in the consecrated phrase. Goethe conceives his Faust as an individual man. The modern age, with its acute self-consciousness and sense of individuality, is clearly reflected in the later poet.

Chapter V

THE POEMS AS WORKS OF ART

In this chapter we propose to take note of a distinctive artistic character which contributes to place the four great poems in a class apart. As regards the artistic merits of the poems individually we make no attempt to cover the ground which has been explored for centuries past in a wealth of literature.

In considering these poems as works of art, we are brought up at the outset against an obstacle which has prevented many modern readers of poetry from appreciating them at their true value. This obstacle must be frankly faced, if the whole enquiry is not to be confused. Their most obvious feature is that they are poems of great length; and such poems cannot be appreciated, if they are judged on principles applicable only to shorter pieces. If many modern readers experience disappointment, and a sense of weariness, in reading a long poem, that is because they are expecting the impossible. They are expecting that on every page they will find poetry as intense, and as highly wrought, as that of Gray's *Elegy* or Shelley's *Ode to the West Wind*. But a little reflection will show that this intensity and high finish, though appropriate to short poems, would be out of place in long ones. It is in any case beyond human power to maintain such intensity throughout a poem which fills a large volume. But even if human power could achieve it, the result would be intolerable to the reader. A minute elaboration, applied throughout, would be as inappropriate to the scale of such a work as filigree tracery applied throughout the whole of a vast building. If a sense of unity is to be produced, there must be proportion, a balance of parts, variation in intensity, carefully measured coordination, blank spaces, points which demand less attention contrasted with points on which attention is concentrated. All these are essential.

Nor, without this variation and complexity, would it be possible to give the sense of wholeness and comprehensiveness at which the poet aims. If the reader is to receive the impression of the vast variety of life, place must be found for some suggestion, at least, of the small as well as the great, the bad as well as the good, the ugly as well as the beautiful, even of the dull and vapid as well as of the lively and significant.

To read such a poem with appreciation is not an easy task. The reward is great, but the effort is considerable. To appreciate a highly wrought poem on a single aspect of life, a single emotion, a single mood or atmosphere, demands less effort; and modern intellectual habits have encouraged the distaste for effort. The reader would do well to be clear in his mind, before he undertakes the reading of the *Divine Comedy*, for instance, whether he is prepared to make the effort which its appreciation necessarily requires. If he has no stomach for such an enterprise, he had best abandon it. It is a mistake to suppose that he will be adequately rewarded by the isolated pleasures he will undoubtedly find in particular passages, in the 'purple patches'. He can find patches as purple if he lingers over his favourites among the vast storehouse of shorter poems—the lyrics, the odes, the elegies, or even the shorter narratives.

What is contended here is that, if he is clear on this general problem of appreciation, and is prepared to brace himself for the necessary effort, he will find that these great structures can give him something unique in artistic pleasure, something which he cannot find elsewhere.

Mere size, of course, is nothing in itself. Mere complexity is nothing in itself. But the great artist knows how to use both size and complexity to produce effects which could not be produced without them. There is one beauty of simplicity, and another beauty of elaboration. It is not only that the grandeur and majesty of a great and comprehensive whole have power to awaken a unique sense of beauty; it is also a characteristic of such works as these that particular passages gain immensely in impressiveness from the effect of proportion, from their place in relation to the whole. Certain passages in poems such as the *Divine Comedy* stand out in the mind with an extraordinary vividness, which they would not possess if merely read as isolated poems. Compared, indeed, with isolated poems of the same length, they might not seem, as they do, incontestably finer. Why is this? Only because they glow like the high lights in a picture, or stand out like the points of special ornament in a great building. What gives them their significance is the great mass which precedes or follows them. The prayer of St Bernard to the Virgin Mary in the last Canto of the *Divine Comedy*, for example, awakens in a reader, who has read the whole work, a sense of beauty which can only be described as overpowering, because it gathers up into itself the memories of the journey through Hell, Purgatory, and Paradise, and thus seems to breathe, in its simple and grave eloquence, the last and purest flame of human aspiration.

We have recurred more than once, almost inevitably, to the metaphor of architecture. It is with that art that the art of such men as Dante has the closest kinship.

A marble tomb may give as great an amount of aesthetic pleasure as a great cathedral. But it is not the same kind of pleasure. In contemplating the cathedral for the first time, the sense of confusion predominates. The mere physical difficulty of seeing the whole, except from a distance, is partly the cause of this confusion. The field of human vision is too small; the fringe, or periphery, of half-vision must be allowed time to impress itself on the eye, until it is familiarised by the frequent shifting of the gaze from one point to another; and thus the deficiencies of the eye can be remedied by the increasing vividness of the imagination. Until this process has advanced some way, the eye can but travel in mere wonder over the lines and shadows and colours. The vast complexity of detail is at first almost overwhelming; the spectator is weighed down by the sense of his littleness, his inability to grasp the whole.[1] Gradually the long process of loving examination begins to reveal the underlying unity. Each part begins to gain significance from its relation to the whole. The impression of strength is heightened by the contrasting impression of delicacy. The huge mass presents itself as the embodiment of the builder's thought, the mason's skill, and the labourer's toil. The consciousness of the spectator's littleness gives way before the consciousness of achievement, as he succeeds in discerning the purpose of each component element. The awe inspired by the initial mystery becomes the abiding awe which attends upon a colossal manifestation of human power.

It is thus with the great poems which comprehend in one view the life and destiny of Man. And yet the metaphor is, at least in one respect, inadequate. The material in which architecture works is stone, or things akin to stone. The material in which literature works is language. The difference is immense. Stone, with all its beauty and variety of texture, weight and colour, points the mind to nothing beyond itself (though the work wrought in it can of course do so). But language is a record of all man's past efforts to understand his environment and to make himself at home in it. It enshrines the thought of past ages. Hardly a word but carries with it some train of associations. And of many words it may be said that they

[1] See A. C. Bradley on 'The Sublime'.

are epitomes of whole spheres of thought and evoke, consciously or unconsciously, memories and images derived from their past uses. All this is apart from the fact that human language contains in itself varieties of musical beauty which are infinite. No small part of the art of poetry consists in so using the associations and the music of individual words, that they contribute their utmost value to the new artistic creation. It is an art of which Virgil and Milton, in particular, are supreme masters.

Chapter VI

THE HISTORICAL VALUE OF THE POEMS

I

There is little danger, in our time, that the historical aspect of the poems will be neglected. The danger is rather that we may emphasise it too much at the expense of their literary aspect. This is due partly to our general interest in 'origins' and 'evolution', to which the nineteenth century gave so great an impetus. But it is due also to the fact that, for quite different reasons, interest in the long poem as a work of literature has declined. Poetry means, to most of us, short poems. Not expecting great pleasure from the long poem as such, the modern reader tends to turn with all the more interest to the many sidelights which it throws upon history. This tendency is increased by the practice of commentators, who find it easier to record ascertained facts than to deal with debatable questions involving critical judgment. The historical aspect of the poems has been minutely studied by scholars. To many minds, indeed, it seems to afford the chief reason for studying them; and some, perhaps, whose taste for history is strong, and to whom literature as such means little, may be wise to take up Virgil or Dante entirely for their historical interest. Many students have in fact devoted a lifetime to this aspect of one or other of the poems. Even within that restricted field, they find themselves fully rewarded by the fascination of their subject.

This tendency of our time, while good in itself, involves the danger that the true appreciation of poetry may be lost. For the perspective of the two studies is wholly different. The historian must give space to each detail in proportion to its historical importance—in some cases, to its mere ·disputableness—and not in proportion to its significance as an element in the poem. We must judge such details by another test, if we are to understand the essential and distinctive value of a work of literature. Dante must not be mainly thought of as a repository of information about the thirteenth century in Italy.

Who—to take a single illustration—who was the Greyhound (the *Veltro*) in the first canto of the *Inferno*? It is a fascinating problem. The Greyhound is the destined Saviour of Italy—the man who is to hunt down the She-wolf (Avarice) now devouring the land. Dante's political conceptions and hopes, at the time of writing, may be revealed by the answer to this enigma. Was it Pope Benedict XI? Was it Can Grande della Scala, Dante's friend and patron? Was it Uguccione, the leader of the Ghibelline party? But while we are making up our minds on this problem, the action is moving; the canto is crowded with important things—Dante's age, the state of mind when he began his journey—the moral obstacles that nearly caused him to turn back—the first meeting with Virgil, his destined guide—the promise of Beatrice's aid to lead him through Paradise. The whole shape and proportion of the poem are being outlined; it is a synopsis of all that is coming. And so in a hundred other cases. To give as much attention to a single historical detail, however interesting, as we give to more essential matters is to shift the focus. Better miss the meaning of a few names than miss the right appreciation of the whole poem.

This, however, is not to belittle the value of the historical knowledge which these poets give us. The light which they throw is ample.

Virgil, for example, has always been accepted as essentially the poet of the Roman Empire in its first inception. In his whole-hearted acceptance of the Empire, he was truly representative of the majority of Romans and Italians of his time. Great as were the traditions of liberty at Rome, the tragic disintegration of the past century—the Civil Wars, the horrors repeated and intensified, the economic collapse, the moral decay—had so disgusted the people that few regretted the disappearance of the ancient Republic. The almost universal feeling was the desire for peace and security at any cost.

This is not surprising when we read what had gone before. At first there had been a social issue at stake. The brothers Gracchus had championed the cause of the poor. It was complicated by a second issue, the conflict of Roman citizens with unenfranchised Italians. Among the Roman citizens themselves, the senatorial was ranged against the popular party. But the perpetual wars—with revolted provinces, with the kingdoms of Pontus, of Armenia, of North Africa—brought great generals to the front, and real issues became the mere catchwords or banners of a raging partisanship. Marius, Sulla, Crassus, Pompey fought for personal power and glory. Twice, in the Triumvirates of 59 B.C. and 43 B.C., a truce between the rival leaders had been attempted; twice it had broken down. The land of Italy went out of cultivation. Civil war broke out in the streets of Rome itself. The very foundations of public order were barely saved, (it was believed), by the defeat, due to Cicero, of the widespread conspiracy of Catiline. Commerce was ruined in the Mediterranean by fleets of marauding pirates. Cruelty to the defeated party reached depths hitherto unknown. Political enemies were proscribed by the successful leader. The rising of slaves under Spartacus, in the year of Virgil's birth (70 B.C.), was a fierce Jacquerie on the side of the oppressed, an orgy of blood on the side of the Government; two thousand crucified slaves lined the Appian Way. Meanwhile the idea gained ground of a coalition of the

East (comprising the main sources of raw materials and food), organised to overwhelm the West. First Pompey, and then Antony, tried to realise this idea. Julius Caesar defeated Pompey at Pharsalia in 48 B.C.; Augustus defeated Antony at Actium in 31 B.C.

The great battle of Actium was felt on all hands to be an epoch-making event. It meant, first and foremost, the establishment of peace and security; that was what it stood for, in the eyes of the common man. But to Virgil it meant the ending of an age of unspeakable horror; the final blow for civilisation. Scholars have been puzzled by the fact that the famous picturing of Roman history, in the scenes engraved on the Shield of Aeneas, dwells at what seems disproportionate length on the battle of Actium. No politician will feel any surprise. In point of fact, it was followed by two centuries of order and skilled administration throughout the Mediterranean world.

For the common man, the idea of the Roman Empire found its personal embodiment in Augustus. It took the form of what is commonly described as 'deification'—in reality, something less simple and definable than what that word expresses, something suggested, no doubt, by the common practice of the Greek cities, which at an early date began to erect temples in honour of the living Emperor, but deriving its real force from the vague Roman idea of the *Fortuna Urbis*, which it was easier to picture in a person than in an abstraction. Perhaps the nearest modern equivalent is the Japanese idea of the Mikado as the 'Son of Heaven'.

To Virgil also the embodiment in the person of Augustus had reality. The man who struck the great blow at Actium was, in his eyes, transfigured. Even before that date, and long before the official 'deification' (which was effected after the Emperor's death, by a formal decree of the Senate)—and indeed in the first of his more famous poems, *Eclogue* i—he calls him *deus*. It was Augustus (then known as Octavian) who had restored him to the beloved farm, from which he had been evicted in 42 B.C. to make room for one of the veterans of Antony's army. 'Oh Meliboeus! 'Twas a god who wrought for us this peace— for a god he shall ever be to me.' Freedom, he says, 'cast her eyes upon me'. He travelled to Rome, and never 'shall that face of his fade from my heart'.

The acquaintance thus happily begun ripened into a close friendship—so close that we may, at least, conjecture that the poet had some part in formulating Augustus's views. Actium was in 31 B.C. Octavian became Princeps, and received the title of Augustus in 27 B.C., the year from which we date the foundation of the Empire. In 29 B.C. Virgil had read aloud to him the *Georgics*. For the rest of his life he was writing the *Aeneid*, and he read aloud to the Emperor and his family Books ii, iv and vi (the central book). It was the Emperor with whom he was travelling when he died.

It is not without significance, therefore, that his hero Aeneas is, in one of his aspects, Augustus. It is an un- questionable portrait; and what is more remarkable, a prophetic portrait. For Virgil died (19 B.C.) when Augustus was only forty-two years of age; and Augustus was to live to be seventy-five. His great work was not completed till A.D. 14. During his remaining years he was to become more and more like Aeneas—oppressed by his gigantic task, never buoyed up by illusions, but clear-eyed, patient, laborious, and above all inflexibly loyal to his Stoic faith, a soldier who would not desert his post.

There are several elements in the *Aeneid* which are designed to further Augustus's policy. Reference has been made previously to the *Georgics*, of which the political object was to support the policy of settling small farmers on the land, and to glorify it by enshrining in verse a

subject hitherto treated by the Romans in prose—the art
and science of agriculture. In the *Aeneid* the policy of
reviving religion, and particularly the old local Italian
cults, and the ancient memories of the land, was furthered
by that profusion of traditions, of names and incidents, of
persons and places, drawn from national history and local
topography, which has made Virgil a valuable source of
evidence on comparative religion.

When we ask why all this seemed so urgent to him,
we have to remind ourselves of his state of mind. He did
not know, as we know, that Augustus would found an
empire that would last for four centuries, and then, though
overthrown, would leave its impress on the Western world
for many centuries more, under conditions which could
not in his time be even conceived. What he knew was that
Rome had lived through a hundred years of anarchy.
Would she slip back? It was on the cards. He knew only
too well that everything slips back to disorder, that farms
go out of cultivation, that simple pieties decline, unless
the forward movement is sustained by constant faith and
labour—just as truly as the boat slips back on the stream
unless the oarsman plies his stroke with unceasing vigour
and vigilance—'thus it is fated that all things become
worse, subside, are carried backward'—

> Sic omnia fatis
> In pejus ruere ac retro sublapsa referri.
> *(Georg.* I, 199.)

We pass now to Dante. He is an 'original authority'
on many facts about the public life and family histories
of the Italian cities on which no other source of information exists. But apart from this, almost every canto of the
Divine Comedy serves to illustrate the external course of
events. Dante himself was intimately concerned with
politics. In his case, indeed, as in the case of Milton, it

would not be too much to say that it was politics that changed him from the solitary and sensitive poet into the mighty poet-prophet that he became—politics that determined, in short, the whole bent of his genius, as it ultimately took shape in the greatest of his works, the *Divine Comedy*.

Dean Church, in his well-known *Essay on Dante*, (written in 1849), disentangled with great skill, and much picturesque description, the confused threads of North Italian politics in the thirteenth century. From such books as his the ordinary reader may gain a vivid idea of the outward world in which Dante lived, and by which the course of his eventful life was determined.

The political theory which dominated that age was the unity of the civilised world under two heads, themselves responsible to God—the Pope responsible for the spiritual life, the Emperor responsible for the secular life, of mankind. But a rivalry had arisen between the two which affected the whole political horizon. Since the days of the great Hildebrand (Gregory VII, Pope from 1073 to 1085), the partisans of the Pope had acquired the name of Guelph, and the partisans of the Emperor the name of Ghibelline. Each encroached upon the theoretical field of the other. The Guelphs were the supporters—not by persuasion only, but by all the crude and violent methods then open to them—of the 'progressive' elements in the city governments, of municipal independence, of the freedom of Italy from the domination of Emperors from beyond her borders. The Ghibellines, not less brutally, stood for strength and unity, both within and without, for the great feudal nobles of the country, and for the integration of cities and country alike in the great structure of a European community under the aegis of the Holy Roman Empire.

Dante was, broadly speaking, a Ghibelline. The case for the Imperial party, as he saw it, was stated by him in his *De Monarchia*. Strange as it may seem, the whole *Divine*

Comedy has been held by some serious Italian scholars to be, in effect, a Ghibelline pamphlet.

After 1265, when the Imperial house of Suabia was decisively defeated at the battle of Benevento, Florence was dominated entirely by the triumphant Guelphs. But these soon divided into the Black Guelphs and the White Guelphs; the city was torn in two by the followers of the Donati and the Cerchi, the one party aristocratic, the other more bourgeois in its sympathies. Dante, like the rest of the Ghibellines, sympathised with the latter; and when they were finally crushed, and in their turn proscribed, Dante was exiled, with many more. It is worth adding that the Black Guelphs enjoyed the support of Boniface VIII, the Pope to whom Dante frequently refers, and whom he condemned to infamy in his *Inferno*. Dante plotted for a while with the White Guelphs, but eventually left them; and all the rest of his life was that of a solitary wanderer and thinker. He died in 1321 at Ravenna.

The reader who studies the poems carefully finds himself impelled, quite irresistibly, to learn more of the background of events against which they stand out; and this takes him much further afield than the events directly illustrated. As a single example of these tempting bye-paths, let us take the appearance of Manfred in the *Purgatory*.

As Dante and Virgil approach the slopes of the Mount, they meet with the crowd of the excommunicated, who, though they repented of their sin before they died, nevertheless must wait, before entering Purgatory, thirty times as long as the time they lived in contumacy of Holy Church. Only one of these is singled out; and to him a long passage is devoted. It is Manfred. We are told in a note that he was the last of the Suabian dynasty of Emperors, and was defeated and killed at the battle of Benevento, in 1265, by Charles of Anjou, king of a territory half as large as modern France. Struck by the interest which the poet obviously feels in him, and the familiarity with all the circumstances of his life and death which the reader is assumed to have, we can hardly read on until we have explored further. We learn that he was the illegitimate son, by an Italian mother, of the extraordinary Frederick II, who collected the artists and philosophers, Jewish and Moslem as well as Christian, at his court in Sicily, and gloried in a complete emancipation from the intellectual fetters of his age, anticipating the heyday of the Renaissance. Manfred, only twenty-two years old, became Regent on behalf of the infant Emperor, allied himself with the Saracens, defeated the Papal troops, made himself King of Sicily, and gained a great position in Italy as the champion of the Ghibelline party. The Pope excommunicated him, and called in the French. The story of Manfred leads us on to an interest in one after another of the great Imperial house of Suabia, whose stately tombs enshrine their memory in the Cathedral of Palermo.

Evidently the handsome features, the proud and princely character of Manfred—'fair, handsome, courteous in aspect'—

> Biondo era e bello, e di gentile aspetto—

had deeply impressed the imagination of Dante. We are told that he invented Manfred's belated repentance—unwilling, perhaps, to consign to damnation so young and magnificent a prince. As with other characters who thus impressed him—Francesca, Ulysses, Cacciaguida—he puts into the mouth of Manfred some of his great lines of universal application:

> Ma la bontà infinita ha sì gran braccia
> Che prende ciò, che si rivolge a lei . . . .

But infinite Goodness hath such wide arms that it accepteth all that turn to it.   (*Purg.* III, 122.)

Per lor maladizion sì non si perde,
Che non possa tornar l' eterno amore,
Mentre che la speranza ha fior del verde.

By curse of theirs [the Church] man is not so lost, that Eternal Love may not return, so long as Hope retaineth aught of green.   (*Ib.* 133.)

The light which Dante throws on history seems brighter and fuller than that thrown by the other three poets, mainly because, for their times, many more sources of information are in existence, or at any rate many more that are familiar to the average serious reader. It does not occur to us to look for such illumination—except on points of detail—from Virgil, or from Milton; while in *Faust* we have a poem so strictly related to subjects of universal interest that it throws little more light on the outward events of Goethe's time than on those of any other.

Of Milton, however, a little more must be said. It is only by a study of his stormy political years (1642–60) that we understand how it was that the poet of *Comus* became the poet of the great epic. Milton was what Tennyson finely called him, the 'God-gifted organ-voice of England'. Professor Masson tells us that in 1651, when the *Defence of the English People* was published, it was observed that the two agencies which had co-operated most visibly in raising the reputation of the Commonwealth abroad were Milton's books and Cromwell's battles. It was no idle boast of Milton's, when he wrote in the Sonnet to Cyriac Skinner, four years later, that he had lost his eyesight

> In Liberty's defence, my noble task,
> Of which all Europe rings from side to side.

Nor can we ignore the part which Milton played in formulating those principles on which all the political 'Liberalism' of Europe has since been based.

But *Paradise Lost* itself has a significance in relation to
the time at which it appeared. After allowing for some
unorthodox features which were peculiar to Milton himself, we find in it a broad outline of the creed of European
Protestantism, as it emerged—for the first time clearly
defined, and militant—after the welter of the Reformation,
the Catholic Reaction, and the Thirty Years' War; the
creed which, side by side with more mundane motives,
inspired the vast European designs of our William III,
and triumphed, after his death, at Ramillies and Blen-
heim.

II

Hitherto I have accepted the customary view of history.
According to Lord Acton, no mean authority, the 'essential basis of history' is 'the external course of public events'.
And this has meant, in the practice of historians, at least
up to very recent times, political and military events. In
the last century, it is true, the conception has widened, and
the ground which 'history' covers has been extended some
distance into the fields of sociology and of economics.
But 'history' proper is still regarded as something separate
from the history of literature, for example, or the history
of religion; if these are referred to, it is in a subordinate
or supplementary chapter, suggesting that they are not,
strictly speaking, 'history'. Of such subjects as these it is
assumed that separate 'histories' should be written.

If, however, we were to take a more comprehensive
view of the significance of history—and one more in
harmony with the mental attitude of our four poets—we
could not rest satisfied with the customary conception.
It would prove to be far too narrow; and, by its narrow-
ness, distorting. It would be impossible to confine history
within such limits. History is the record of all that has
happened to man in the past. We should crave for a more

connected picture. Nay, more; we should begin to construct for ourselves a new scale of values; we should place the history of thought and feeling, in the order of importance, above the history of 'outward events'; at least if we accepted—as the present writer accepts—the view that man's actions are determined primarily by his ideas and emotions, not by some iron necessity imposed on him from without.

The highest place in our scale would be given to the development of religious and other conceptions; to the influence of guiding or of originating personalities; to man's efforts and achievements in the cultivation of all his powers, in the creation of works of art, in the elaboration of social living. The last of these general headings would include, of course, those political events which the existing practice of historians has accustomed us to regard as 'history'; the organisation and inter-relation of communities, of states, and of empires. It would include also that mechanism, or outward shell, of civilisation—the aeroplane and the radio—which, to the popular mind, seems to constitute civilisation itself, but which we should place in due subordination to more important things. All these would be but parts of the general picture which the historian would present to us—a connected picture, with all its proportions duly observed. We still await such a presentation.

In such a picture the separation between 'History' on the one side, and 'Literature', 'Social Life', 'Art' or 'Religion' on the other, would cease to have any meaning. All these departments of life, without exception, would then form part of the historic whole. It would then be inappropriate to say that our poets 'throw light on history', as if they occupied a position outside it. We should rather say that they, and their poems, were themselves history; were indeed among the most important of 'events'. From this standpoint it would be more appropriate—to take a single instance—to say that Charles II came to the throne shortly before *Paradise Lost* was published, than to say that *Paradise Lost* was published in the reign of Charles II.

In what way then are our four great poets, Virgil, Dante, Milton and Goethe, a part of history? Briefly and generally, it might be answered that, if they had never existed, the story of Man's past would have been something different from what it was.

Let us remind ourselves that we are not primarily judging the merit of their work from the aesthetic standpoint, nor testing its truth or its value at the present day. We are asking simply, what is the significance of these poets among the innumerable phenomena of the past?

First and foremost, of course, they created works which rank among the outstanding achievements of the human spirit; milestones, as it were, along the road whereby the Western mind has come to be what we find it to-day; high-water marks by which the achievements of others were measured; models which stimulated the ambitions of posterity. They provided channels in which production, and the taste of readers, afterwards flowed. Their personalities impressed themselves on the imagination of Europe, and touched hidden springs of feeling, latent susceptibilities, which added to the emotional wealth of later times. As a personality, a poet like Virgil is something more than an interesting and instructive witness. He is an authentic voice, speaking to us out of the past.

In their four great poems, each presenting us with a picture of the Universe as a whole, they gather as in a focus the broad tendencies and general intellectual conditions of their respective ages. We learn from them the extent of the knowledge then possessed, and its limitations; the point of view from which the chief problems of life were regarded; the light in which both the past and the future appeared; above all, the things which were then held to 'matter', and those which were not. Such poets do not of course tell us these things in so many words; the things are implied by their choice of one subject rather than another, one set of ideas rather than another. They give us personal stories, particular allusions, for the sake of their individual interest; but in so doing they bring out, unconsciously, a general framework of thought.

Yet they are, at the same time, far from being mere mirrors or microcosms of their times. The view of life which they present in a synthesis of their own, moulding and combining anew, becomes something different from what it was; and even their contemporaries, though it seemed to them familiar, were in reality learning something new. The greatness of such men consists in the fact that they go far beyond their time. They realise intensely its essential character. They feel its melancholy weakness and pettiness; yet they feel its potentialities also; consciously or unconsciously, they summon it to rise to the height of what is in it. Often disregarded in their time, they come slowly into their kingdom generations afterwards.

Virgil, for example, gave expression to the ideas and emotions which lay behind the policy of Augustus—purified and harmonised, of course, but still the real operative forces. A certain parallel may be found in the relation of Milton's ideas to Cromwell's policy. In each case the writer put into words the thoughts about politics which animated the leader, and which woke an answering chord in the minds of thousands of educated men. The conception of a world-state embracing, but not suppressing, all the peoples of the earth was, not indeed the first, but certainly the greatest, of the political ideas given to the world by our Western civilisation. Compared with this, the idea of a 'national' state was a mushroom growth arising from the peculiar conditions of the fifteenth century.

Seen in the light of the recent events of that time the reasons for Virgil's underlying political ideal become clear, even obvious. The things that seemed to him to matter were precisely the things which, in the past century, had been gradually lost, the things whose loss meant the decline of true civilisation. It is on what he conceives to be the essentials of civilisation that he constantly dwells. Among these, political order stands first. But it is not a political order founded on mere superiority of force; now that peace is restored, there must be generosity instead of vengeance, reconciliation in place of perpetual enmity. This is the significance of the final reconciliation of the Trojans and Latins, after their long and savage war, in Book XII of the *Aeneid*.

What makes for order, again, is not the mere will of a monarch, however disinterested, but the spirit of reverence for law. The citizen must accept, too, the principle of steady, purposeful, constructive labour, of which the life of the Italian farmer is the type. And fundamentally, order rests on the moral qualities of *gravitas*, seriousness and a sense of responsibility, and *pietas*, the sense of duty, the respect for observances, for the past, for the ancient loyalties and usages which are the growth of ages, and yet are so easily and quickly undermined.

Virgil is constantly preoccupied with all that distinguishes the civilised from the crude and barbarous. In the Elysian Fields, side by side with the heroes and prophets, are the men who 'by the invention of the arts refined our life'—

Inventas aut qui vitam excoluere per artes.

It is impossible to translate *excoluere* by one English word. It contains the ideas of tending a garden, of protecting and of adorning, as well as that of refining. *Colo*, of course, is the verb from which comes our modern expression 'culture'. Virgil gives us a view of things which was doubtless shared by many Romans who cared about philosophy; it resembles that of Cicero; but it is primarily his own slowly built-up conception of the world. We have to remember that the thinkers of Rome were primarily moralists, not metaphysicians. Based on his passion for order, for law, for civilisation, his system embodied the stern ethics of Stoicism—more and more to become the real religion of Rome—but it also went beyond ethics, and conceived the universe as penetrated by one divine spirit; and individual souls as corrupted by their contact with matter, and then, after their life on earth, purified through long ages of purgatorial cleansing till they entered upon life once more. Here we go back to purely Greek sources, to Plato and Pindar, and to Pythagoras, whose doctrine was introduced to Roman thought by Poseidonius in the preceding generation. Virgil's earlier Epicureanism, we may suppose, had proved untenable to him during his close contact with public life, through Augustus and Maecenas.

Virgil's personality, too, is a matter of history. His refined, gentle and retiring nature, combined with his wide culture and his intense seriousness, and embodied for ever in a consummate work of art, carried his influence through century after century; in the Dark Ages men began to regard him as one who became a Christian before Christ, and also as a potent magician; innumerable legends sprang up around his name. But the real man could be recaptured, as long afterwards as the thirteenth century, by a poet like Dante, 'searching his volume' with eager love—

> Vagliami il lungo studio e il grande amore
> Che m' ha fatto cercar lo tuo volume—

and in Dante's pages he lives again. If he meant so much to Dante, he must have meant something, at least, to hundreds of less famous thinkers.

I turn now to Dante. The *Divine Comedy* stands out above the other three poems by the completeness with which it gives expression to the general conceptions of an age. The imaginary date is 1300. The actual writing took place between 1312 and 1321. Dante had mastered the whole field of knowledge then accessible. But this alone would not suffice to justify placing him apart from the others in this respect. Virgil's mastery of the knowledge of his time was probably not less complete. The difference is that the age of Dante itself, unlike Virgil's—or indeed Milton's or Goethe's—possessed an intellectual synthesis which rendered it more possible to present a connected impression of the whole. It was easier to summarise than theirs. The mind of Europe then moved within an accepted scheme of things—that of the Mediaeval Church. The scope and limits of its thought were laid down with a precision unknown to other ages; and moreover Dante was born in the century—the thirteenth—which was also the century of St Thomas Aquinas (1227–74). Aquinas, in his *Summa Theologiae*, worked out, in a systematised form, an explanation of the world, and of human knowledge, which gained almost universal acceptance.

It incorporated not merely the Church's view of things in a limited sense, but also the essential thought of the ancient world. The fact is momentous; it touches the basis of our Western civilisation. It was no small matter that Christianity, when it was first being formulated as a system, did not cut itself off from the intellectual heritage of the ancient Hellenic, or Hellenistic, world. It was due in the main to the Greek Fathers of the Church—above all to Origen (A.D. 185–254), who worked in Alexandria and in Palestine—that the Catholic Church did not take the course which it might well have taken under the influence of less liberal Latin Fathers like Tertullian (A.D. 155–222) and Jerome (A.D. 340–420). The merits of the course adopted may be disputed; from time to time great thinkers, like Calvin at the Reformation, and Professor Karl Barth in our own time, have presented a view of God according to which all human effort, however lofty or noble, is worthless and unavailing for salvation; but the fact remains that the early Church recognised two great contributions to the *preparatio Evangelii*, the stream of Jewish ardour and vision, and the stream of Greek and Greco-Roman thought and science. For Aquinas placed Reason side by side with Revelation as one of the twin sources of truth; and his rational scheme was founded on the logical and metaphysical works of Aristotle. It is this which enabled Dante to accept the culture of the ancient world, as far as it was known to him, whole-heartedly and without any sense of impropriety; to mingle classical and Biblical persons in his examples of virtue and vice; to address Apollo as 'Father'; to take Virgil (in one of his aspects) as the representative of Human Reason, and as his 'teacher' and 'leader', his guide through Hell and Purgatory. His conception of the Earthly Paradise is that human wisdom and virtue, unaided by Revelation, can lead man to a certain perfection, which he reaches at the summit of the Purgatorial Mountain; it is the identical garden which Adam and Eve inhabited before the Fall. It was part of God's purpose that man should attain this perfection as a stage on his way to the Beatific Vision of the Heavenly Paradise.

Yet, in spite of this wide door opening into antiquity, the cosmology of the Mediaeval Church determines, in large measure, the boundaries of Dante's thinking. The Earth is the centre of the Universe; it contains in itself both Hell and Purgatory; around it are the spheres of Air and Fire, then those of the seven Planets, then that of the Fixed Stars, then the Primum Mobile, and beyond that the Empyrean, or Heaven, where there is neither Time nor Place. These are the walls of Dante's world—in the arresting phrase of Lucretius, the *flammantia moenia mundi*.

When all is said as to his representative character, it remains true that in many respects Dante is daringly original. He stands out above all poets by the proud and defiant self-reliance which disregards all literary models; by his epoch-making decision to discard the Latin language, and to be the first European to use the vernacular for a serious and ambitious poem. Moreover, in his moral judgments, and in his estimate of the importance of this or that individual, he follows no guide; he pronounces with absolute and unfettered independence—whether in the ruthless severity of his condemnation, or the discriminating insight of his praise.

Both Virgil and Dante, in their day—it is especially true of Dante—represented a party. And this, it must be admitted, impairs in a certain degree their representative character so far as concerns those ideas which underlie politics—their ideas, that is to say, concerning the fundamental conceptions of government, of law, and of justice. The same is true, perhaps in an even greater degree, of Milton. He represents the ideas of Protestantism. *Paradise Lost*, both in the religious and the political ideas which inspire it, is a representative picture of the things that mattered in the world of Protestant Europe. We cannot forget, however, that the Catholic world, too, claimed the allegiance of millions, and had its own deep springs of emotion and action, towards which Milton's attitude was one of mingled dislike and contempt.

Within that Protestant world, and above all in England, the influence of Milton's personality has been lasting. It is no small matter that the spirit of Puritanism found its supreme expression in one who perpetuated it in its most persuasive shape; whose mind dwelt naturally, not on its narrow or crabbed or fantastic elements, but on its lofty sense of responsibility; at the same time giving full value to culture, to science, to beauty, to the wisdom and eloquence of the ancient world. Wordsworth's Sonnet, 'Milton, thou shouldst be living at this hour', is only one among the many impassioned testimonies to the magnetic power of his personal character, in its combination with high artistic achievement.

What, finally, of Goethe? His achievement was, in the main, an individual and solitary achievement—a landmark in the story of the human spirit, a supreme example revealing unknown potentialities. If we ask how far he is representative of his age, the question must be answered in two different ways. If by 'age' we mean the whole modern age, which we may date roughly from the French Revolution, through the times in which we now live, to an end we do not know, then it may be said that he came nearer than any other man to combining in a single work of art those essential features which, as far as we can judge, differentiate it from the ages of Virgil, of Dante, or of Milton. But this is a matter rather of the present time than of history.

On the other hand, if we mean by 'age' a more limited period, with more precise features, defined already by students of literature and sociology, we shall find much truth in the description sometimes given of Goethe, that he represents the Humanism of the eighteenth century. This is largely true; and in so far as it is true, it means that he represented a period which was past at the time of his highest and most characteristic production—a period in which he lived for forty years, but which he also outlived by forty years. The description corresponds, none the less, with some of the most striking aspects of his achievement. Three of these may be mentioned; his eager curiosity for, and his desire to coordinate and comprehend every form of human activity; his critical, but fundamentally Deist attitude on religion; and his belief in an enlightened and benevolent autocracy, as being the best political ideal. The first recalls Diderot and the Encyclopaedists; the second, Voltaire (if we allow due weight to the garden-temple at Ferney, with its inscription *Deo erexit Voltaire*); the third, the rule of Joseph II of Austria.

To the end, these retained their hold as guiding principles in all Goethe's production. It is perhaps in the last that he is most representative, for here his eighteenth-century ideal was not displaced, even by his broad-minded understanding of wholly new political currents. It is clearly illustrated in the closing Act of *Faust*. Goethe is seeking for a means of symbolising the highest stage of development that Faust reaches in his earthly life. Faust, by far-sighted planning and dictatorial organising of labour, reclaims land from the sea, and so builds a basis for the life of a people—not free from the difficulties and dangers which form character, but free to work (*tätig-frei*) and free from want. In the contemplation of this prospect, he can conceive of that satisfaction with the moment—'Oh stay, thou art so fair' (*Verweile doch, du bist so schön*)—which he had sought all his life in vain. He has a glimpse, for the first and only time, of what it means to live in and for the whole; there is the vision of the free people, and in their life he lives. 'Aeons may pass, but the traces of my days on earth cannot perish.'

> Es kann die Spur von meinen Erdetagen
> Nicht in Aeonen untergehn.

(Faust ii, Act v, Sc. 7.)

But just as Goethe's life extended far beyond the period of the eighteenth-century Humanism, so his mind travelled into regions which would have seemed unfamiliar, and indeed outlandish, to a Diderot, or a Voltaire, or a Joseph II. He developed far wider conceptions of religion, of the scope of scientific knowledge, of the place of beauty in the ascent of civilised man. In literature, he felt the first thrills of the Romantic Revival, and then reacted strongly against what he regarded as its excesses. He appreciated to the full the new passions for Freedom, for Democracy, for Fatherland, for which men around him were striving and fighting and dying, and though he could not share them, he never ignored their profound significance.

He lived on into a wholly different age—an age of bewilderments, of gigantic struggles, of great achievements followed by great disappointments. He framed his own synthesis, but it was not one which could claim to be representative of such an age, whose chief characteristic was that it could not accept any synthesis whatever. Viewing him in this light, we are at a point where the present dominates the scene, and the recent past is merely ancillary to it. The age he pictures is, in essence, our own age; we still live in the midst of it. The ideas that take shape in *Faust* constitute the intellectual and spiritual environment with which we ourselves are familiar. This is why the reading of *Faust* does not give us the sense that we are learning history. But the men of future ages—those who, to use Dante's phrase, 'will call this time ancient' (*che questo tempo chiameranno antico*)—will turn to it as the work of art which best gives expression to what, in our day, we call the scientific spirit—its restless questioning, its inability to accept any 'system' or 'scheme of things', its extreme self-consciousness, together with its new aware- ness of the unconscious, its distraction amid innumerable objects of interest, its vain attempts to master and control the machinery it has invented.

Chapter VII

THE MORAL AND INTELLECTUAL
EFFECT OF THE POEMS

The subject to which we now pass on is one more difficult
to describe, but it has even more importance for our main
theme. I refer to the general effect which the study of
the four great poems produces on the mind, and especially
on our intellectual outlook and moral attitude. This effect,
it will be contended, is different in kind from any which
can be produced by works of a narrower scope and aim.
It is bound up with, and inseparable from, the fact that
they aim at presenting a picture of life in all its essential
aspects. In a short chapter, however, we cannot do more
than open out certain lines of thought which may prove
suggestive, and cull a few illustrations for our theme.

It is worth noting, at the outset, that the intellectual
and imaginative effort, which is required to appreciate
such poems, is not a small one. For that very reason,
however, it affords an invaluable training for the mind.
To attempt, at any rate, to grasp the main features in so
wide a view is a corrective for the modern evil of specialisation—or more generally for the evil of splitting up our
attention among innumerable separate objects—the vice,
in particular, of a popular culture so largely based on
newspapers. The writer who calls upon his readers to make
such an effort is facing a formidable task; he is calling
upon them to renounce the prevailing intellectual habits.
Yet the effort is worth the making, and this chapter is
designed to show what we gain from it.

No doubt much may be gained, and is gained, by the
knowledge of particular parts or passages of these works.
It is better to know the debate of the rebel angels in Hell

than to know nothing of *Paradise Lost*. But the reader who knows no more of such works than this must completely fail to profit by what is really distinctive in them. The writers conceived their works as wholes, with a single main purpose. This purpose was what moved them to write; they made it their life's work to embody it in a great work of art. Their peculiar distinction, and the core of their achievement, is the process of fusing and unifying the experience and thought of a lifetime, by which their purpose was carried out. It is this from which all their other similarities flow. And it is the overruling purpose and the genius shown in a special mode of fulfilment which bind these four, as it were, in a brotherhood of greatness— reminding us of those 'four mighty shades, lords of the loftiest song', whom Dante met in the underworld, and to whose company Virgil, and Dante himself, were added.

Hence it is all the more to be regretted that in our own time—whatever may have been the case in former days—leisure is seldom found for the study of these great poems as wholes, their chief significance and the object of the poet himself being thereby lost.

Perhaps the first effect of reading them in their entirety is the unique sense they afford one of seeing a vision of human life *as a whole*, not only in its present but in the past and in the future, not in one country or continent but universally. We see Man's life on earth, from the point of view both of what the writers conceive to have happened before, and of what they conceive to happen afterwards. We live in the presence (to use Browning's phrase) of 'the wonderful dead, who have passed through the body and gone'.

By this comprehensiveness the poems bring us up against the main problems which the thinking man or woman has to face. They compel us to ask—has life a meaning? Of what nature is the unseen world, if such there be? Are there any absolute standards of value? What are the place and destiny of the individual and what, if any, is his responsibility? Is his will free to choose this or that course? And what is his relationship to his fellow-men? Must he submit himself to the restraints of law, and if so, for what purpose and within what limits? The achievements of civilisation which distinguish Man from the animals—his political structures, his works of art, his apparatus of scientific knowledge, his technical conquests of Nature, his social institutions, his methods of education—are they good, or bad, or indifferent, when seen from the point of view of the whole? Assuming that he has a goal, are they leading him nearer to the goal? Has there been, or is there to be, progress in history?

We find ourselves impelled to look on these questions not merely as separate problems, but as parts of an all-embracing survey. The scene is panoramic.

In their manner and power of giving this total impression of life the poet-prophets differ of course widely. Dante and Goethe show certain elements which are lacking in Virgil and Milton. Thus we find in them more humour and more variety; in particular a special readiness to give due place in their picture of man's life to the repulsive, the undignified, the grotesque. Again, Virgil and Milton give one a less direct sense than Dante and Goethe of the range of their interests and knowledge. But on the other hand in the course of telling their stories they are supreme in the introduction of those simple and powerful phrases which arrest us by the universality of their application—phrases which cause the gulf of centuries to disappear and make us feel that the problems which the poet had to face are those of our own world too.

In each one of them we find the deep seriousness, passing at times into the solemnity, which attends a far-reaching view of things. They call upon us to throw off the mental bonds which tie us to life's innumerable details in all their deceptive importance, and to view things afresh in the light of a larger whole. We have to remember that each of the poets in turn played an active part either as a man of action or as a writer in a critical period—in some cases a turning point in history—when it had become clear to him how great were the issues shaping themselves for the weal or woe of mankind. His imagination was wrought upon by direct contact with dark and sordid realities of life; they gave him cause to wrestle intimately with the most fundamental problems of evil and of sin, and thereby to qualify himself for the true role of poet-prophet. In each of the poems the poet has embodied his own philosophy of life (an incomplete one in the case of the most modern as of the most ancient—although Virgil in early days was often called 'the Plato of poets'). In each case we see that he has arrived at a stern ethical ideal. It is of great interest to trace these ideals in the four poems and to compare them.

At the time of writing their greatest works, the minds of Virgil, of Dante and Milton in turn were still overshadowed by the grimmest pictures of civil war. (Dante was born five years after the disastrous battle to which he refers in the *Inferno*, 'the havoc and the great slaughter which dyed the Arbia red'.) This fact lends all the more impressiveness to their hopes for the future and to their faith in the possibility of human progress. In the popular religion of Rome, the *Aeneid* came to fill the place of a sacred book setting forth and upholding, as no other book did, the relation of men, and to a special degree of Romans, with the Higher Powers. The hero of the *Aeneid*, (at any rate in his final development), embodies Virgil's moral ideal of self-mastery, fortitude and courage in carrying out the Divine Will, a Will which demands devotion to justice and to the tasks of civilisation. But the note of the poet-prophet is one of sadness as well as of seriousness. Man can learn to endure, but there is little room for joy. His life here and hereafter remains wrapped in uncertainty and mystery. And although Virgil himself represents the ethical ideal of Dante, and 'the sea of all wisdom', the man chosen to guide his steps to the very threshold of Paradise, Virgil is debarred from crossing the threshold, which is open only to those who have received the higher wisdom of Revelation. 'In His Will is our Peace', are the words Dante puts into the mouth of Piccarda, the serene voice speaking from Heaven. The sense of 'freedom in obedience', of joy in it, and security marks the Christian outlook of the poet-prophet, who nevertheless in his pre-Christian predecessor finds 'his sweetest father'.

What a foremost place 'justice' occupied in Virgil's mind (as later in Dante's), and its association for him with the Divine scheme of things is clear from many allusions. In Hades the horrible fate is indicated for us of those who, for personal reward, misused the laws, or helped to impose 'a tyrant lord' upon their country, and wretched Phlegyas cries out continually in the gloom: 'Be warned, learn ye to be just and not to slight the gods', (*Discite justitiam moniti et non temnere divos*). Virgil's ideals were influenced by the Stoics, for whom the rule of Reason, (coinciding with that of Virtue), found its basis in the idea of the universe as a Divine Whole, and of Mankind as an essential unity in which the individual could realise his true self. Man in fact was 'cosmo-political', designed to form one community with one common law, (hence the achievements of 'Roman Law'), a 'City of Zeus' or universal *communis deorum et hominum civitas*. In the later poet-prophets these ideas are to be traced, influencing, and blended with, what is specifically Christian. The ideal of a World Empire, which Virgil extolled, and helped to create, represented one of the first great political conceptions of the Western World. It was the Roman Empire which gave the foundation for the political philosophy of Dante. It embodied the conceptions of order, impartial justice, a common law for all peoples, and of unity and peace between them, in which he could still find most conspicuously 'the footsteps of God in the world'. In the material empire he saw, moreover, the type and precursor of the spiritual empire of the Holy City.

We have discussed the difficulty of determining at what points in their own minds the line was drawn by the poet-prophets between literal and symbolic truth. What is certain is the necessity they felt to gauge the mind of the great public they wished to reach, the degree of spiritual truth this public was capable of receiving, and the forms—pictures, allegories, myths and symbols—which could best convey it. Dipping, however, further below the surface, it is their constant sense for the same underlying spiritual truths which impresses us. Thus their ideal for the individual is only to be found in association with that for a larger whole, the State, and behind the State, humanity.

Both Dante and Milton attested their sense of political responsibility most strongly in their personal lives. It plunged Dante into the struggle between Guelph and Ghibelline. It led Milton to that height of self-dedication and sacrifice which for nearly twenty years meant laying aside the role of a poet for that of a political fighter. Such service was to him a matter of religion.

The effects on Milton of the prolonged political struggle were profound; it largely determined—it would not be too much to say it deflected—the ultimate direction of his genius. The joyous young poet of *Comus* was changed by his voyage in the 'troubled sea of noises and hoarse disputes', and came to view things in different perspective. Evil and sin appear as the dominating problem of life; he makes us realise them as something momentous, sinister and horrible. As he contemplates them even his style tends to become bald and bleak. We need to remember too that the Restoration, which seemed the shipwreck of all his work and hopes, brought his own life into immediate danger. It was spared, and he was able to settle down to the task of poet-prophet. In the light of his own past experiences we feel the poignant reality of his words. Thus the ideal of loyalty to Truth is enshrined for ever in the description of Abdiel, who had just made reply to Satan:

> Among the faithless, faithful only he;
> Among innumerable false, unmoved,
> Unshaken, unseduced, unterrified
> His loyalty he kept, his love, his zeal;
> Nor number, nor example with him wrought
> To swerve from truth, or change his constant mind
> Though single....

(P.L. v, 896.)

The phenomena of the mass-mind, so familiar to us now, remained to be explored by the psychologists of centuries to follow. But we can feel that Milton, three centuries ago, had just the same experience, and perhaps fuller consciousness of what the ugly thing means in practice, with all its degrading compulsions. He thoroughly understood how the gregariousness of men leads to the domination of reason by passion.

The doctrine of Free Will and the reality of individual responsibility presented itself to Milton, as also to Dante, as a most vital issue; whereas by Virgil and again by Goethe it is simply assumed. When the irrevocable parting comes between Dante and his 'beloved teacher' who is debarred from Paradise, we may note the final words of Virgil's impressive farewell. He himself 'can discern no further', but Dante's preparation for Paradise is now complete:

> Libero, dritto e sano è tuo arbitrio,
> e fallo fora non fare a suo senno:
> per ch'io te sopra te corono e mitrio.

(Purg. xxvii, 140.)

('Free, upright, and whole, is thy will, and 'twere a fault not to act according to its prompting; wherefore I do crown and mitre over thyself'). With these lines we may compare Milton's in the last solemn warning of the Archangel Raphael to Adam:

> Stand fast; to stand or fall
> Free in thine own arbitrement it lies.
>
> *(P.L.* VIII, 640.)

Milton's ethical ideal is one of proud independence of ordinary human motives and obedience to God alone—to live 'as ever in my great taskmaster's eye'—with acceptance of all things adverse 'without distrust or doubt'. Some of the ideas to which Virgil in his succinct manner devoted here and there a significant line or two, or perhaps merely hinted at, are in Milton given full and flowing expression. Thus the seemingly disparate ideas of obedience and power, of service and liberty, are to be found associated most clearly by Milton.

> Who best
> Can suffer, best can do; best reign, who first
> Well hath obeyed—.
>
> *(P.R.* III, 194.)

Those are Kings and Conquerors who rule their own passions, desires and fears, and are prepared for Truth's sake even to suffer death. He who fails to reign 'within himself'

> ill aspires to rule
> Cities of men, or head-strong multitudes,
> Subject himself to anarchy within,
> Or lawless passions in him which he serves.
>
> *(P.R.* II, 469.)

The conception of liberty as depending on something within man which he must himself develop, and as attained only by those who subdue their lower natures; the true meaning in fact of outward 'freedom' and its necessary limitations had become very clear to Milton. Liberty was something which could not really exist except in closest union with certain other things: 'true liberty'

> which always with right Reason dwells
> Twinn'd, and from her hath no dividual being.
> Reason in Man obscured, or not obeyed,
> Immediately inordinate desires
> And upstart passions catch the government
> From Reason, and to servitude reduce
> Man till then free . . ..
>
> (*P.L.* xii, 83.)

The judgment of God then subjects men to tyrants— 'violent Lords'. When nations 'decline so low from virtue, which is reason', that they lose their inward liberty, then

> justice, and some fatal curse annexed,
> Deprives them of their outward liberty.

Even Virgil expresses something of this view of 'true liberty' in King Latinus's reception of the invading Trojans, to whom he declares the Latins to be 'Saturn's race, righteous not by bond or laws, but self-controlled of their own free will and by the custom of their ancient God'. But it is the nature of 'Mammon', as Milton says, always to reject a 'splendid vassalage' to God, and rather to seek

> Our own good from ourselves, and from our own
> Live to ourselves . . .
> Free, and to none accountable.
>
> (*P.L.* ii, 253.)

'Better to reign in Hell than serve in Heaven', says Satan.

In Goethe we find the idea of true freedom more subtly expressed. When Faust's imagination depicts for him the future scene of 'free men on a soil that is free' wresting their livelihood from land reclaimed from the sea in defiance of the furious flood that beats against the dams, he affirms that word of 'highest wisdom':

> That only he deserves his life, his freedom,
> Who wins them every day anew.
> Nur der verdient sich Freiheit, wie das Leben
> Der täglich sie erobern muss.
> (*Faust* ii, Act v, Sc. 7.)

In these lines as in many others we find an echo of Goethe's favourite philosopher Spinoza, who writes in his *Ethic* that most people 'believe they are free just in so far as they obey their own passions, and that they renounce their rights in so far as they are constrained to live according to the precepts of divine law'.

Throughout the Faust story Mephistopheles may be found playing a role similar to what Milton assigns to 'Mammon', when the latter uses the lure of a freedom which is deceptive and in fact fictitious. The very idea of service and of obedience offends the primitive longing for freedom; the individual life, and civilisation itself, tend to degenerate into an embodiment of Satan's defiance. The devil upholds the importance of the ego, and urges man to repudiate all obligations imposed upon him by the divine Whole which, in reality, controls his happiness and freedom, his own higher nature being bound up with it.

It is worth recalling that Spinoza was the 'God-intoxicated' Jew of the Hague, whose grandfather in the seventeenth century found refuge there from religious persecution in Portugal. The first reading of Spinoza appears to have opened a new chapter in Goethe's life, and gave him the inspiration of a religion. The Stoic idea of the universe, revived and developed by Spinoza, appealed strongly to Goethe:

> How all things weave themselves to one,
> Working, living in each other.
> Wie alles sich zum Ganzen webt,
> Eins in dem andern wirkt und lebt!
> (*Faust* i, Act i, Sc. 1.)

To Spinoza, and in turn to Goethe, the unity between all men, though 'veiled from common sight', was in fact as real as the opposite idea of separateness is 'real' to man still under the spell of his senses. Once we can rise above the sensuous consciousness, of which Mephistopheles in Goethe's presentation is the consistent champion, we move towards the realisation of the true self.

This higher knowledge, however, is attained only in conjunction with the action which accords with it. Goethe reflects this idea in the primal importance he gives to *Die That*. "Thus Faust's love for Helen (who typifies classic beauty) is contemplative and 'ideal' but out of it is born a spirit which drives him back into the 'real' world of action" (*Goethe and Faust*, Stawell and Dickinson, p. 201). In this harmony of thought with action is to be found the highest peace (though outward peace be lost), and man attains the only freedom which is real.

In the finely balanced life of an idealism which is inseparable from outward struggle, Spinoza had stressed the part to be played by imagination, had urged even the habits of speech which dwell rather upon human virtue and perfectibility than on 'vices and impotence'. Men were to unite themselves 'by bonds which make all of them as one man'; and 'minds are not conquered by arms but by love and generosity'. Spinoza's ideas help us to appreciate the positive, affirmative and striving spirit which breathes through Goethe's work. His practical ideal was the life lived in the Whole as well as in the Good and the Beautiful—different aspects in reality of the same thing.

> Im Guten, Ganzen, Schönen
> Resolut zu leben.

The ideal was nothing unless embodied in the actual, and this must be done in defiance of the 'Spirit who still denies' all that is born of man's higher self. Goethe mistrusts everything which might lead men 'away from activity in the outer world to a false inward contemplation' (Stawell and Dickinson, p. 15).

In the character of Faust we find no embodiment of an ethical ideal, such as Aeneas was to Virgil. Faust may rather be taken to represent the struggling spirit of a full humanity. He is the all-round human being who, with a thirst for knowledge and experience, drinks deep of the wells of life's interest and pleasure; a thorough-paced sinner, but one who learns and strives. Faust's wager with Mephistopheles consists in this: That all the devil's delights, flatteries and lies will never lure him into satisfaction with the life of sense. Mephistopheles hurries Faust from one unsatisfying experience to another. Finally, in despite of him Faust begins to gain the necessary self-mastery and, while continuing to press forward, acquires the power to renounce what had hitherto been irresistible; in the end he rises above his passions. When enthusiasm seizes him for the project of reclaiming land from the sea, this practical enterprise of disinterested idealism marks Faust's truest bid for his own happiness. Mephistopheles resists the project, (which typifies the highest tasks of civilisation), with scorn and rage. But the devil's part is finished when Faust is no longer swayed by the voice of Reason suborned to the service of the senses. At that moment Faust dies; but we learn from the 'angel voices' that he who is 'for ever striving' wins his salvation, though only with the help which comes from the higher spiritual world—what in fact is termed 'grace' in the language of theology (Stawell and Dickinson, p. 252).

Goethe's long life coincided with great changes in the world including, in the French Revolution, one of history's volcanic upheavals in life and thought. Vast new fields of knowledge were opening out. Goethe followed all with the industrious attention, eagerness and sympathy which were characteristic of him. Even for a man, however, of his grasp and universality of mind, the range of interests heralding the modern age had become so wide that the task he set himself was almost impossible. The indication, even faintly, of all he desired in the small compass of the longest poem could often only be done by the briefest allusions. There are many lines in Faust which represent a whole train of thought, and there is no attempt to work them out, as in his reference to freedom earned 'every day anew'. Faust is a *tour de force*, and Goethe is probably the last man of genius of whom it will be recorded that he attempted to cover the whole field of the knowledge of his time, and to embody in one great work of art the ripe fruit of his learning and reflection. He succeeded in so far that it may fairly be said of him, as Arnold said of Sophocles, 'he saw life steadily and saw it whole'. So great was his objectivity that he admired Napoleon and was even ready to have a friendly discussion with him when he invaded Germany. *Voilà un homme!* was Napoleon's tribute to him after this interview at Erfurt. Goethe, in fact, exemplified Spinoza's dictum that 'the brave man will ever seek to remove the hindrances to true knowledge, such as hatred, anger, envy, derision, pride...'.

What is true of the greater problems of life which the poet presents to us is true also of particular thoughts and phrases. Each single utterance—a line or a few lines—takes on a greater significance from its connection with the whole. It fits in, as it were, to a unified conception of life. It may not be, in itself, as perfect in expression as a similar apophthegm in a fable of La Fontaine, or in a play of Shakespeare; but it often seems weightier and more memorable because it is related to, and conjures up before the reader, the outlook on life which inspired the poet; it is instinct with his whole message. It is this which gives its significance to such lines as Milton's

> The mind is its own place, and in itself
> Can make a Heaven of Hell, a Hell of Heaven;

or to Goethe's lines on the nobility of struggle:

> Säume nicht dich zu erdreisten,
> Wenn die Menge zaudernd schweift;
> Alles kann der Edle leisten,
> Der versteht und rasch ergreift.

Be up and do the daring thing while the irresolute crowd are wavering! All things can be achieved by the noble-minded when he has eyes to see and acts swiftly.

(Faust ii, Act i, Sc. i).

When the Arcadian king, in Virgil, welcomes Aeneas to his humble palace with the words:

> Aude, hospes, contemnere opes, et te quoque dignum
> Finge deo, rebusque veni non asper egenis—

Have the courage to despise riches; form thyself, thou too, on the model of the god, and be worthy of him; scorn not our mean estate—

we breathe the atmosphere of sternness and dignity which informs the whole *Aeneid*, because it is the poet's consistent moral attitude throughout.

A striking example may be taken from Dante. In *Purgatory* (xiv and xv) he dwells on the distinction between material goods, which depend for their enjoyment on private possession, and spiritual goods, which are increased by sharing. It so happens that a similar idea is expressed by Shelley in *Epipsychidion*; and in our own day Mr Bertrand Russell has reproduced it with philosophical precision in his *Political Ideals*. Dante's expression is crude and even awkward by comparison; but how much more deeply it impresses us, when we recognise in it the great idea of charity which casts its gleam on the Purgatory, and illuminates the Paradise with its full glow!

O race of men, why place ye your hearts there, where the refusal of companionship is necessary?...But if the love of the highest sphere moved your desire upward, you would not have that fear at the heart; because the more there are by whom 'ours' is said there, so much the more of good each possesses, and the more of charity burns in that cloister.... That infinite and ineffable good which is on high, so runs to love as a ray comes to a shining body. It gives as much of ardour as it finds; so that in proportion as charity extends, increases upon it the eternal goodness. And the more the folk who comprehend one another on high, the more there are to love rightly, and the more love there is, and as a mirror one renders it to another.

(*Purg.* xiv, 85; xv. 52. Butler's translation.)

We have now said enough to indicate the comprehensive nature of the poet-prophets' outlook in their attempt to give an interpretation of life. Some of my readers, however, may still be ready to ask, why is the panoramic view important? Why trouble to give ourselves any connected account of life's problems? Why have a *Weltanschauung*—a philosophy of life—at all? It is a question often put nowadays, especially by younger people—not always consciously or directly, but quite obviously implied in their intellectual attitude towards life, and in their complacent acquiescence in giving themselves no account of it. One cannot ignore the importance of this tendency. Nor can one lightly dismiss it as having no justification. A full discussion of it cannot be attempted here; but a few considerations may be submitted. Such an attitude is in part a very natural result of the increasing hurry of life in our century; its endless distractions and bids for our attention in matters which are either essentially unimportant or must remain so until viewed in a larger setting. In this chaos and clash of minor interests life in a more real sense may be said to have no longer any leisure for itself.

Another important factor is to be found in the influence of the new science of psychology and the stimulus it gives to self-centred thinking. It has certainly helped large numbers of people to acquire an exaggerated sense of the importance of self, of the world within (of our own desires, impulses and tendencies, conscious and unconscious) as compared with the world without. Such a focusing of the mental eye—with the self as the centre of vision on life's canvas—leaves small space for respect or reverence for anything apart from it. The capacity for religious belief or conviction of any kind tends also to be undermined by the lingering idea that psychological, or other explanations regarded as 'scientific', can account for such beliefs, apart from their objective truth or otherwise. In general, perhaps, a vague sense may be found to prevail that the inconclusiveness of science is more to be respected than are the convictions of the world's preachers—or of the world's greatest prophets and poets. Little regard is paid to the part that these convictions have played in building up European civilisation—in so far as it has been worthy of the name.

Whatever the causes of it may be, the mental habit of insistence on the importance of self, which at times has almost seemed to merit the term of a modern disease, certainly constitutes a break in the tradition of European thought which is represented by our poet-prophets, and in large measure is also their creation. What we may call the 'panoramic' view of life undoubtedly seemed important to the poets themselves; or perhaps it may be truer to say that to them it seemed so obvious that they took it for granted. This is equally true of Goethe, by far the most self-conscious of our four poets, who in so many ways anticipates the spirit of our times, and in particular shares to a great degree the modern tendency to and capacity for scepticism. This makes the fact all the more impressive that it never occurred to him to question the value of the attempt at a comprehensive survey of man's life and its problems. Otherwise he would have offered some apology for his 'Prologue in Heaven', which indicates the scope of the whole drama, and introduces Faust to the reader in the same great scene which presents the archangels chanting the glories of creation. He insists on the need for a unified view explicitly in all his speculations; as is not surprising in a disciple of Spinoza, who emphasised the unity of things to a degree which some thinkers consider excessive.

To those, at any rate, to whom this point of view conveys some degree of truth, it must seem a service of high value to accustom both the intellect and the imagination to contemplate the 'kingdom of all the worlds' and to realise that this kingdom and no narrower one is, as a modern novelist has put it, 'the theatre of man's destiny, and the fit measure of his achievements'. That contemplation, and that feeling, these poets help to arouse in our minds in a manner that is beyond the reach of the philosopher. The poet, moreover, heightens our sense both of the evil and of the good; and we feel how finely balanced is the issue between them. At the same time he saves us from one-sided views of truth; for we see things all together, connected and coordinated, not as separated and isolated subjects. We see them in proportion, in their relation to one another and to the whole.

It is this which conveys that tranquillising effect, that strange sense of calm, which is so often attributed to these great works, but so seldom explained. It is due to that consciousness of harmony, which is inevitably felt when apparently conflicting truths are brought together in a comprehensive unity. That pessimism concerning progress, for instance, which is so widely felt at the present time, finds a corrective—if indeed any corrective can be found at all—in a picture which shows us, not the present alone, but the present in relation to the past and the future. Or if we contemplate the problem of evil in all its aspects, we gain at least a fairer view of it when the evil things and the good things of human life are presented to us at one time and in one picture. Pain and tragedy may play the most prominent part in the panorama before us. Nevertheless the voice of despair is silenced; the final note is one of hope.

It is no exaggeration therefore to compare the impression made on us by these poems with that which we gain from contemplating Nature, when from some cliff or mountain we see her on a vast scale, with all the gradations which lead the eye from the smiling homesteads to the barren heights, or the impalpable distances of the sea.

The man who allows himself to be absorbed by these poems, who yields himself to their influence, is not quite the same man as he was before he knew them. This is a matter which can be tested only by experience; but the expressed opinions of men who are recognised as great in literature—and not merely in literature but in the active public life of the Church or the State—form a body of testimony so impressive that it cannot be ignored. What these poems have meant to the leaders of European thought and action may be traced from the days of St Augustine, who shows in his *Confessions* what it cost him to tear himself away from the *Aeneid*, down to those of Wordsworth, who found confidence that 'the flood of British freedom' would continue to flow for us

> who speak the tongue
> That Shakespeare spake; the faith and morals hold
> Which Milton held. . . .

In a survey as brief as I have attempted, it is impossible to indicate the richness and variety of my subject. In conclusion I would like at any rate to submit how great is the loss to culture at the present time that the study of the *long* poem, and above all of the few great 'comprehensive' poems of the world—perennial sources of stimulus and inspiration to the mind of Europe—should have fallen into relative neglect.

Chapter VIII

THE BASIC IDEAS OF WESTERN CIVILISATION

In answering the main problems of life—or at least in facing them—the four great poets give us something which has a special value at the present period in history. For civilisation itself is held by many serious thinkers to be in grave danger. And the poets provide a strong reinforcement for those ideas which underlie it. What exactly that civilisation is, few take the trouble to enquire; though many are prepared to exalt it into the supreme good.

It is fair to assume, at least provisionally, that the main ideas on which that civilisation rests will be found embodied in the comprehensive or 'cosmic' poems in a higher degree than in other works. First of all, these works have in fact been accepted and absorbed by the European peoples. Their widespread acceptance—the influence they have exercised, through literature, on European culture—raises a presumption that they are truly representative in character. But this, it may be said, would be equally true of, say, the Bible or Shakespeare. There are, however, important differences. The comprehensive aim of these poets—a unified picture of human life—in itself compels them to adopt some definite attitude towards life's major problems. And, as I have pointed out in speaking of their historical value, each poet gives us, not mere separate indications, but a connected view of the outlook of the age in which he lived.

Doubtless much careful study is needed to disentangle the fundamental from the superficial, and the ephemeral from the permanent. But the essential ideas are there. The poets do not, of course, present their ideas with the clarity and consistency of a philosophical system. The work of the philosopher is different; he appeals to the intellect alone. The poets present their ideas in another way; they reach the ears of a far wider audience because they appeal to the intellect and the imagination and the emotions alike—in a word, to the whole man.

There is an initial difficulty in formulating these basic ideas. They seem too familiar to be worth expressing. Ideas such as the dignity and importance of the individual man seem at first sight, at any rate in normal times, to be truisms, statements of principle which no one could dispute, conceptions which for generations have been accepted as underlying all civilised life; so completely a part of our particular cultural heritage that most of us can hardly imagine a civilisation based upon others. Looking back, we can now see that this attitude showed an insufficient appreciation of the varied potentialities of the human spirit. In point of fact, these ideas would by no means have seemed self-evident to the men of Ur of the Chaldees, or of Egypt, or of Peru; nor would they seem self-evident now to an educated Hindu, or Chinese, or Moslem. And, to come nearer home, some of them are expressly rejected by the National Socialists of Europe, and also by the Communists.

Let us consider, however, a little more closely what for the present purpose we mean by the word 'basic'. In studying the poets are we to limit ourselves to those ideas which are common to all four of them—including the pre-Christian Virgil? This would be to exclude ideas of which, perhaps, not even a germ could be found in the Graeco-Roman civilisation, yet which must clearly be classed as essential parts of the European or Western outlook. Some, again, would treat as basic such a late-developed idea as that of 'progress' in one or other of its numerous senses; or the idea of nationalism which has acquired, in the modern world, a power which seems for the moment irresistible; or even late-developed institutions, such as industrial capitalism or parliamentary democracy. None of these will here be treated as 'basic', but rather as outgrowths.

We are in fact driven back upon the endeavour to formulate, not recent growths, or the outlook expressed in certain modern institutions, but those ideas which seem to underlie our Western civilisation whenever or wherever they may have originated or developed, and to whatever branch of Man's activity they may relate; those ideas which, if they survived in the minds and hearts of men, would again become the seeds of a new world, similar in its essentials to the world that we Europeans know, even if all our ancient monuments and all our particular institutions were destroyed to-morrow; those ideas which, as Shelley said of the 'foundations of Greece', are

> Built below the tide of war,
> Based on the crystalline sea
> Of thought and its eternity.

It is these ideas which it is really essential to keep alive in the minds and hearts of men. It is only if these were weakened and lost, and forgotten, that we could fairly use so strong a phrase as the 'death' of our civilisation. For they are the root out of which in the end it might spring up again. Infinite disasters might happen meanwhile; but our civilisation would not be 'dead'.

Briefly, European thought has rested on some such fundamental conceptions as these: that the life of man is a good and not an evil, and that it has a purpose, a goal towards which we ought to strive; that there is a spiritual world, independent of Man but to which he is related; its laws create fixed standards which he can discover, of Goodness, Beauty and Truth, by which his works and institutions, including governments, are to be tested; that the individual man, as distinct from the social group, has a nature and destiny which give him dignity, a free will, and with it the power and the duty to strive constantly towards something better. (It is for these reasons that liberty of thought, speech, and action had come to assume supreme importance in the minds of Western Europe.) Civilisation, which opens an ever-widening field for knowledge, thought, experience, and activity, thereby developing personality and helping the individual towards his goal, is neither valueless nor bad, but good. In return, as he cannot live alone, the individual must recognise and respect the laws of some wider whole. What is that 'whole' to be? Humanity as a whole makes an imperative claim, for it contains a common interest which transcends all local or tribal differences. It is in this common interest that the most real and lasting basis for 'justice' is to be found.

Ideas such as the above have influenced the minds of men who were the finest products of Western civilisation, and who in all departments of life have in their turn added to our European heritage. However vague our thoughts are apt to be when we speak of our civilisation, granted we are prepared to dip beneath the surface at all, we shall find that we too are feeling after some such conceptions as these. Other civilisations may hold, or have held, some of the same elements. But taken in combination they form a whole which is unique.

Even this statement, rough as it is, will it is hoped stimulate the reader in his desire for the study of Virgil, Dante, Milton and Goethe. It is not the least of their claims on our attention that they provide us with many a noble assertion, and many a vivid sidelight which bears upon these conceptions; and if we remember the range of their influence, we may place them among those who, to use a modern metaphor, have 'charged the batteries' of European thought. Some ideas, of course, find their most striking illustration in one poet, and some in another; while for certain elements, notably the Christian, we necessarily turn to the later rather than the earlier works. Time has brought its gradual accretions. Each age, each religion, each great forward movement of thought or of experience, has contributed something, and the elements which have formed the basis of our civilisation are Jewish, Greek, Roman, Christian—Mediaeval, Renaissance, Protestant, Modern.

In essentials, I believe that we shall find a consensus among the four poets, perhaps beyond our expectation, as to the things which are held to 'matter', to be our primary concern, to have abiding value. Some of these have been indicated, but special importance may be given to the following: all of them hold that life is good, and to be desired; our purpose, or the purpose of the Universe, is not to escape from it; the goal is not Nirvana. All, as has often been pointed out in the course of this book, recognise a spiritual world, the source of what is highest in each of us, the theatre of our destiny, by whose laws our actions on earth must be tested. All assume, and two of them repeatedly insist upon, the freedom of man's will, and therefore the individual man's responsibility. And all maintain that humanity transcends all differences between men, and that human civilisation is good and desirable, and a part of the scheme of Providence for man.

Dante and Milton insist the most upon both the Transcendence of God, and His Immanence in individual men. The reason is simple. By their time these principles had become subjects of conscious controversy; whereas with Virgil they had not arisen, and with Goethe they had ceased to arouse any passionate interest. The unanimity on this point of the spokesmen of Catholicism and

Protestantism, otherwise so sharply opposed, is notable; both alike are in the true tradition of Christendom. It is Christendom, of course, that first gave to European thought both the consciousness of its unity, and in the Holy Roman Empire an organisation which embodied it. Milton, it may be added, is perhaps even more keenly conscious than Dante of the Transcendence of God, perhaps even of the supreme and awful primacy of the laws of the spiritual world; but on the other hand the idea of the Immanent God—the Son of God is often identical with the Reason, dominant over Passion, which is the spark of the divine in man—is at the very root of his philosophy.

In Virgil we have the doctrine *deum ire per omnes*, the *caelestis origo*; while Goethe, in one of his best lyrics, suggested by Giordano Bruno, writes:

> Was wär' ein Gott, der nur von aussen stiesse,
> Im Kreis das All am Finger laufen liesse!
> Ihm ziemt's, die Welt im Innern zu bewegen,
> Natur in sich, sich in Natur zu hegen,
> So dass, was in ihm lebt und webt und ist,
> Nie Seine Kraft, nie Seinen Geist vermisst.

What sort of God would it be who worked only from the outside of things—just set the world a-rolling on its own! Rather must He move the world from within and preserve Himself in Nature, while Nature preserves herself in Him; thus everything that lives and moves and has its being in Him shall never lack His power nor His spirit.

It is perhaps on the issue, 'Has human civilisation a value or has it not?' that the consensus is most striking. We need to realise how intensely vivid this issue seemed to the early Christian teachers. With us, the answer 'It has' has been regarded as obvious; it was challenged by Calvin among others; and in recent years the issue has once more become vivid; Professor Karl Barth has impressively answered, 'It has not'.

To help in this realisation of its vividness, I propose to cite two examples. St Jerome was a lover of Pagan literatures; the language of the prophets seemed to him 'rude and uncultured' (*sermo horrebat incultus*). He describes in his letters how, in a dream, he found himself before an almighty Judge who said to him, 'Thou art a Ciceronian, not a Christian; where thy treasure is there shall thy heart be also. What has Virgil to do with the Gospels, or Cicero with Paul? We cannot drink the cup of Christ at the same time with the cup of those who worship demons.' Jerome replies, 'Lord, if ever I possess secular books, and read them, I deny Thee' ('*Ciceronianus es, non Christianus; ubi enim thesaurus tuus, ibi cor tuum...Simul bibere non debemus calicem Christi et calicem demoniorum.' 'Domine, si unquam habuero codices seculares, si legero, Te negavi'*).

The second is from the time of the Counter-Reformation. In *John Inglesant* De Cressy speaks thus:

'You have been taught all that men desire to know, and are accomplished in all that makes life delightful. You have the knowledge of the past, and know the reality of men's power, and wisdom, and beauty which they possess of themselves, and did possess in the old classic times;....You have culled of the tree of knowledge, and know good and evil; yea, the good that belongs to this world, and is part of it, and the strength, and beauty, and wisdom of the children of this world; yea, and the evil and ignorance and folly of the children of light. Let us grant—I am willing to grant—that Plato has a purer spiritual instinct than St Paul. I will grant that Lucretius has the wisdom of this world with him; ay, and its alluring tongue. Paul did not desire spiritual insight; he wanted Jesus. You stand as a god free to choose. On the one hand you have the delights of reason and of intellect, the beauty of that wonderful creation which God made, yet did not keep; the charms of Divine philosophy, and the enticement of the poet's art; on the other side, Jesus. You know Him, you have seen Him. I need say no more of His perfections....

'I offer to you nothing but the alternative which every man sooner or later must place before himself; shall he turn a deaf ear to the voice of reason, and lay himself open only to the light of faith? or shall he let human wisdom and human philosophy break up this light, as through a glass, and please himself with the varied colours on the path of life? Every man must choose. You wish this life's wisdom, and to walk with Christ as well, and you are your own witness that it cannot be. . . .'

He saw the path of perfect self-denial open before him—renunciation, not of leisure, nor even of the world, but of himself, of his intellect, of his very life—and distinctly of his free choice he refused it.

(p. 201.)

With Virgil and Goethe, the value of human civilisation is simply assumed. Virgil looks on it as the main goal of human life, and the very substance of history. Goethe devotes the Second Part of *Faust* very largely to the true foundations of civilisation, and particularly the part played in its development by Beauty, personified in Helen, and Ugliness, personified in the Phorkyad. But Dante and Milton had boldly faced the terrible issue that was so vivid to Jerome and De Cressy. They knew that the case for denying the value of human culture, represented mainly by that of Greece and Rome, was a powerful one from the Christian point of view. Among the Early Fathers of the Church (with whom Milton was even more familiar than Dante), the issue had hung in the balance. To Origen (A.D. 185–254), more than to any other, was due the happy decision which saved the old culture for Christian men. Thenceforward it became, with Jewish culture, one of the twin streams which moulded the Catholic tradition, and thus passed into the heritage of European civilisation. How shattering the sacrifice would have been to Dante is vividly suggested by his choice of Virgil for his guide. The old civilisation, so inexpressibly dear to him; the warm, familiar, human beauty of it; all this was summed up in his beloved poet. He took full advantage of his liberty, and mingled classical and Biblical heroes without the least sense of incongruity.

In Milton's day, human culture was once more being put in jeopardy, under the powerful impact of Calvinism on the Puritans. But Milton's was fundamentally a Renaissance mind, and he belonged to the earlier school of Puritanism which had no idea of rejecting culture. His whole philosophy of life, based so largely on the Immanence of God in man, supported the wider view. Yet the temptation must have been strong; and once, but only once, in the strange denunciatory words spoken by Jesus in *Paradise Regained*, one is given cause to wonder whether Milton himself had yielded to it—perhaps under the dreadful spiritual shock of the ruin of all his hopes at the Restoration of 1660.

Whatever the significance of the above passage it is still true to say that the poet-prophets show a degree of consistency as regards the basic ideas which cannot fail to impress us. Life on earth presented itself to them as part of a larger whole which gave it purpose and value; they saw our life, in fact, against the background of a spiritual universe, the laws of which were in reality conditioning our fate.

If the poet-prophets were justified in believing this spiritual world to exist, it involves consequences which in the present as in the past go down to the roots of our civilisation. It demands the steadfast maintenance of certain fixed criteria by which our life on earth must be judged. Goodness and beauty are not the chance preference of this or that man or age. Theories, works of art, governments, empires, all alike are to be brought before the bar of a court which cannot be tricked or evaded; whose judgments cannot be bought with a price; and which admits of no appeal.

In his brilliant little book, *La Trahison des Clercs*, M. J. Benda has given to all those who uphold standards of truth, beauty and goodness 'in opposition to the realism of the multitudes' the name by which the Middle Ages described the man of education as opposed to laymen— that of the *Clercs* ('Clerks'). These standards and the principles of humanity and of justice derived from them, as opposed to the mere dictates of men's passions, were on the whole upheld till towards the close of the nineteenth century. It is true that the *Clercs* could not restrain 'the laymen from filling all history with the noise of their hatreds and of their slaughterings'. But at least the *Clercs* 'prevented such things being turned into a religion'. For 2000 years, thanks to them, mankind, while committing evil, did at least honour the good, thus 'creating the breach through which civilisation could find a way'.

But towards the close of the nineteenth century there came about a radical change: the *Clercs* themselves began "to play the game of political passion; they who had held it in check became its instigators, and the flatterers of its servants; men of letters, artists, philosophers, theologians, descended into the arena of national hatreds and of political faction; they became the prophets of 'sacred egoisms'". Is this wholesale adoption of 'realism' to be final or temporary? asks M. Benda; does it herald the advent of an age far more barbarous than the former Middle Ages, and if so may we hope for a "new Renaissance, and a return to the religion of Disinterestedness"? His answer is pessimistic. At best it could not happen for a long time to come, not in fact "till war should have caused the world far more evils than it has so far". It is significant that Benda's book was published twelve years before the second World War.

Of the *Clercs* in M. Benda's sense, Virgil, Dante, Milton and Goethe stand out as conspicuous leaders. They are, one and all, prophets of the *disinterested activity of the spirit*; expecting and demanding, with regal assurance, the recognition of its supreme value.

We have then the support of M. Benda for the view that the threatened collapse of our civilisation is due to the weakening and loss of those underlying ideas which were far more real to generations gone by. It is not difficult to trace some of the causes of the loss. The progress of science basing itself upon exact material evidence inevitably gives rise to doubt as to the reality of all that lies outside its own vast field. Again, the tendency of the Mechanical Age has been to entangle the individual in an elaborate machinery of outward life, which is apt to sweep him away from access to its real springs. His sense of proportion too suffers as a result of intensive technical specialisation; attention is often concentrated on the details of some infinitesimally small corner of the map of life, while the map as a whole with the names writ large across it may not be seen at all. The mental outlook in such a case presents the opposite extreme to that of the poet-prophets, who cultivated to the utmost the power of seeing details in the light of the whole. From various aspects it may thus be seen that what for many decades past has been accepted as 'civilisation' has ceased to develop and tended rather to suppress the individual personality. In so far as this was the case, civilisation had lost its true function and also its power of survival.

It is war time which introduces the supreme test of our standards and of the 'basic ideas' on which they rest. When life and civilisation are felt to be at stake, we soon realise that a man's familiarity with 'basic ideas' affords no measure of his real faith in them. Some seem to have survived for him as mere social conventions—a Sunday attire to be thrown off when need is felt to get down to some real work. Such ideas as the universal Fatherhood of God and the fundamental identity of human interests are left to haunt the pulpits, and do so less and less; it takes a bold preacher to express their implications. Individual life and its values must perforce cease to count; and whole categories of men for all intents and purposes cease even to be regarded as human. In this connection also we should not underestimate the psychological re-action of war technique on the millions of men who carry it out; every month of war adds to the number of those practices which in themselves are a negation of the very ideas on which civilisation (in so far as it was worthy of the name) had gradually been built up.

If the 'Death of Europe' has become a phrase which haunts the mind, it is due to developments such as these, which must be admitted to have profound spiritual significance, with results more far reaching than can yet be foreseen. One of these may be mentioned here: the widening of the field for superstition in measure as the capacity for moral conviction has been undermined, and conditions have become unfavourable to independent and serious thought.

Civilisation again is endangered not only from the attack of opposing ideas, but from the collapse of order over wide areas, and sheer pressure of immediate material needs (which may continue for a long period to come); the same process which brought on, little by little, the so-called 'Dark Ages' following the collapse of the Roman Empire in the West. We must reckon too with the fact that in-security and hunger create the imperious demand for order at any price; the dictatorship, which may avail to restore it outwardly, at the same time destroys liberty of thought, and the vicious circle of destructive processes begins anew.

> . . .facilis descensus Averno. . . .
> Sed revocare gradum superasque evadere ad auras,
> Hoc opus, hic labor est.

. . .How easy the descent to Avernus. . . .But to recall one's steps and to escape once more into the upper air, what a task! What toil!

Why should we assume, as most people seem to do, the survival of our civilisation? Such civilisations as the world has hitherto seen have been a rare and ephemeral product in the history of mankind, carrying within themselves the seeds of their own decay. It is possible that our Western civilisation may also prove to have been short-lived and that another Dark Age is imminent.

Early in the sixth century, when the Roman Empire was· approaching its end, two great men, ministers under Theodoric the Goth, discerned the coming danger. Immersed though they were in the duties of office, Boethius first, and Cassiodorus some decades later, laboured to prepare some little ark of learning whereby the seeds of enlightenment and culture might be saved from the rising flood of barbarism. Boethius, by translations and commentaries, strove to bring the inspiration of Greek thought to his countrymen, and to enshrine the knowledge of his time in works on science and the arts. At the same time, this 'last of the Romans', in his position as Consul, sought to preserve the former Roman standards of justice. This resolute resistance to evildoers procured him many enemies; he was accused of plotting against Theodoric (his intimate friend), imprisoned and cruelly put to death at the age of forty-four. But Boethius had turned his 'necessity to glorious gain'. In the prison cell he wrote *The Consolation of Philosophy*, described by Gibbon as 'a golden volume, not unworthy of the leisure of Plato or Tully, but which claims incomparable merit from the barbarism of the times and the situation of the author'. This is the book to which Dante turned when death robbed him of Beatrice, and there are many lines in the *Divine Comedy* which seem to echo its passages.

Cassiodorus retired early from his public position to carry on work in the monasteries which he had founded for the purposes of his mission. Under his supervision the monks copied and translated manuscripts which were to hand on the most important knowledge, both sacred and profane, for the use of future ages.

It is the spirit of these two men, men of action, but equally men of learning and insight, which our world needs. They were public servants *par excellence*. Our situation offers a certain parallel to theirs.

Let us not fail, when suffering under the stress of irreparable loss, to view the future in such light as the past may afford. The four poets whose work is the theme of this book were above all great Europeans. They are the best spokesmen of our Western civilisation. In so far as it has been a true civilisation, the ideas which have been formative of it are to be found embodied in their works. It is civilisation in this sense, and this alone, which makes our sacrifices worth while, and for ever demands our service—the thing which it is incumbent upon us, whatever the disasters of our time, to cherish and preserve for those who come after us.

AENEAS TO HIS FRIENDS

Dear Friends, whose courage oft ere now was tried
By perils bravely fronted, side by side,
Courage once more! To these too God shall send,
As once to those, his own appointed end.
What, ye who dared to face the echoing den
Where raging Scylla gnawed the bones of men;—
Ye, comrades, ye, whose stout hearts did not fail
When rocks Cyclopean round us fell like hail,—
Shall we fail now? An end to craven fears!
Perchance e'en woes like these, in after years,
With pleasing thoughts our memory shall employ,
And sorrow be transmuted into joy.
Keep firm your hearts, keep fresh your strength, for we
Shall need it in the better days to be.
Still, still, in vision seen, ordained of fate,
The Latian fields our wandering steps await;
There shall we build in peace the hallowed towers,
And raise anew the Troy that once was ours.

Aeneid I. 198–207.
(Translated during the first World War by C. R. B.)